MW00427183

EVERY

MOVE

MATTERS

Every
Move
Matters

UNLOCKING VALUE IN
LIFE AND REAL ESTATE

Vickey Barron

Forbes | Books

Published by Forbes Books, Charleston, South Carolina.
Member of Advantage Media.

Forbes Books is a registered trademark, and the Forbes Books colophon is a trademark of Forbes Media, LLC.

Printed in the United States of America.

10 9 8 7 6 5 4 3 2 1

ISBN: 978-1-95588-472-3 (Hardcover)
ISBN: 978-1-95588-473-0 (eBook)

LCCN: 2022923872

Cover design by Matthew Morse.
Layout design by Matthew Morse.

This custom publication is intended to provide accurate information and the opinions of the author in regard to the subject matter covered. It is sold with the understanding that the publisher, Forbes Books, is not engaged in rendering legal, financial, or professional services of any kind. If legal advice or other expert assistance is required, the reader is advised to seek the services of a competent professional.

Since 1917, Forbes has remained steadfast in its mission to serve as the defining voice of entrepreneurial capitalism. Forbes Books, launched in 2016 through a partnership with Advantage Media, furthers that aim by helping business and thought leaders bring their stories, passion, and knowledge to the forefront in custom books. Opinions expressed by Forbes Books authors are their own. To be considered for publication, please visit **books.Forbes.com**.

In loving memory of my mother.

Acknowledgments

I wanted to take a moment to express my deepest gratitude to the following people who have been instrumental in my writing this book.

To my husband, Lenny, Thank you for being my rock, confident, and biggest cheerleader. Every time I wanted to quit, pause, or give up on this book, your words of encouragement and belief in me was the strength, support, and love I needed to see it through. Your unwavering support has been the backbone of my writing journey, and I am so lucky to have you by my side.

To Larissa Petrovic and Pacey Barron, Between taking care of our clients and closing deals, you both found the time to help me edit this book! Your countless insights and suggestions helped me shape my work into something truly special, and your support was needed to see this project through. Thank you for not quitting on me. Your contributions have been immeasurable, and I will be forever grateful to both of you.

To Laura Mercier, You have not only revolutionized the cosmetic industry but highlighted the importance of confidence, self-care, and authenticity. You and your brand have encouraged me and countless others to embrace our unique beauty, which has had a profound impact on our self-perceptions and the way we approach life. I'll never forget the day we spent packing up your kitchen when you were gracious enough to walk me through your beginning years as an artist deciding which direction to take. Your story is a testament to the importance of trusting your gut, hard work, perseverance, and creativity. I am grateful to know you and all that you stand for. Thank you for your contribution to my book and, more importantly, my life.

To Robert Reffkin, I want to express my sincere gratitude for your outstanding contributions and support to the entrepreneurial community. Your vision, passion, and persistence has inspired countless entrepreneurs to pursue their dreams and strive for success. You continue to outline what it takes to make a dream a reality. With deepest respect and admiration, thank you for dreaming big and for your remarkable leadership.

To Barbara Corcoran, I want to express my appreciation and thank you for inspiring me and many others. Your impressive career in the real estate industry and your commitment to empowering others in business has also motivated me to raise the bar. Your persistence in shows like Shark Tank has been not only enlightening but also entertaining. Your clever wit and astute business acumen are always on full display. I've learned so much from watching you in action, and I am a better entrepreneur/marketer because of your example. You have set an extraordinary standard of excellence for others to follow, and I know that your legacy will continue to inspire countless others for years to come. Once again, thank you for sharing your wisdom, talent, and passion with the world. It has been a privilege to learn from you.

To Leonard Steinberg, I want to take a moment to thank you for your incredible contributions to the real estate industry and for the daily words of wisdom you share with all of us. Your knowledge, creativity, and cleverness have helped shape so many of us into better professionals. Your insights have shown us that there is always room for growth, that we should never stop learning, and that we must always challenge ourselves in order to achieve success. These lessons have been invaluable to us, and we can never thank you enough for your generosity and support. Imagine what the real estate world would look like without Leonard Steinberg. As we continue to move forward in our careers and life, we will always carry your wise words with us. Thank you for being an inspiration and a mentor, Leonard. You are truly appreciated by many.

To my team, I want to express my deepest appreciation for all the hard work and wisdom each of you has contributed over the years. Your expert guidance and dedication have been invaluable in helping me build a brand and a following in real estate. I cannot thank you enough for your unwavering support and outstanding commitment to our shared goals. Together we have accomplished something truly exciting and special. I feel so fortunate to rely on your skills and expertise and feel blessed to call each of you a member of my team. To Jennifer Lafferty, as the longest-standing member, your contributions have been absolutely invaluable, and I will never forget the many late nights when you worked tirelessly supporting our clients and me. I cannot imagine achieving our team's success without you. And to Teka Barron Klopfenstein who contributed to our team for many years and has successfully joined Compass as a realtor in California.

Foreword

In today's fast-paced and rapidly changing world, it's easy to get lost in the shuffle. With so much information and competition around us, it can feel impossible to make a meaningful impact in our personal and professional lives.

Vickey Barron knows firsthand how hard work and determination can pay off. Her book chronicles her humble beginnings being raised by a single mother to succeeding in the rough waters of New York City real estate brokerage. I can attest, this is not easy, especially if you have not lived in the city prior to starting your career.

Contrary to the false narrative that successful agents are dreadful, self-serving, and overpaid, Vickey proves that likability, knowledge, and determination often go hand in hand with success. I'll be perfectly blunt: there was a time when I simply did not believe that Vickey Barron was genuinely as nice as she appeared, and I pondered whether her niceness was forced. I was proven 100 percent wrong. Over the years, our industry had made me jaded and skeptical. And suspicious of everyone. Vickey's likability is infectious, and it's truly who she is. Is she tough? You bet! Is she a thorough professional? Yes. Is she perfect? She would be the first to admit she is not, which makes her even more likable.

In her book, Every Move Matters, she harnesses everything she has learned over the years to provide the reader practical advice, real-life examples, and insightful observations. You'll learn how to ask the right questions, discover new insights, and achieve greater success in all aspects of your life. Confidence, competency, and kindness—without arrogance—are very likable qualities indeed.

Vickey is no pushover either: far from it. She is a tough negotiator and a shrewd strategist. Behind her appealing facade is an astute brain and genuine strength. It's not just about the big decisions we make but also the small choices we make along the way that can have a significant impact on our journey. By following her guidance and advice provided in these pages, you can become a more effective leader, a better decision-maker, and a positive force for change. The icing on the cake is the relationships you'll foster. I highly recommend this book to anyone who wants to make a difference in their industry, organization, or community. Every move matters, and the insights and guidance provided by the author can help you make the most of your opportunities and create a better future for us all.

LEONARD STEINBERG
Chief Evangelist and Corporate Broker, Compass

Contents

"How Did I Get Here?"

After hearing all my stories over the years, some people have encouraged me to put the stories together and write a book. My life reminds me of a Spielberg movie—so many crazy, terrifying, and amazing things have happened to me during my time on this planet (sometimes all at once), but no matter how weird things get, they fortunately seem to turn out OK.

At the same time, as one of the top real estate brokers in New York City, several agents have suggested I write a book about my approach to life and real estate.

I give talks and teach a lot of seminars as a way to give back and share my knowledge with others, so I meet a lot of agents—some who are just starting out and others who have been in the business for years—all searching for the secret to succeed in what can be an extremely competitive field. And every time, they come up to me with the same questions: "Why isn't what I'm doing working? What part of the picture am I not seeing? What do I need to do to be successful that I just can't figure out?"

So my dream was to write a book to share some of my stories, along with something about my approach to life (which isn't always the most orthodox), with the goal of answering some of those questions agents always ask me, and maybe offering a little hard-won wisdom at the same time. It would be light. It would be fun. But at the same time, and, with any luck, it would be inspiring.

And then the pandemic hit.

And suddenly everything felt a whole lot more serious.

During the pandemic, the entire world changed—and my world, the real estate world, was no exception. The economy was in flux, prices were all over the place, and people had no idea how to think about the future. Even the way we did our job changed, and it continues to change. How do you adapt a profession that's been all about personal contact to a world where meeting face-to-face might make you sick? People were afraid—more than I've ever seen before. Nobody knew when or how this would end or how things would change—never mind how to deal with the reality.

And yes, that included me.

But while I was, admittedly, unsure of where this was all going, I was not actually afraid, as I believe each chapter in our life serves a purpose. Maybe that's why this whole experience has actually inspired me. Of course, I am crushed by the death and the suffering that has affected so many people (including my own family members). But I also saw this moment as an opportunity to take a pause and just breathe. Everyone is always so busy, running around doing things. Who has time to take stock of ourselves and how we approach life and *how* we do things? Well, for many of us, time was a commodity that's suddenly more available. So while we're addressing these larger problems that have shaken our world, what if we took this as an opportunity to think more deeply about how we treat each other, how we treat the environment, and equally important, how we treat ourselves? What might be different when we come out of this?

That's why I knew we could get through this. It's a matter of mindset with people, process, and passion.

I guess that, if anything, has been the real secret to my success. If I can do that, maybe I can help you find it too.

• • •

Honestly, success was the last thing that anyone (other than myself) expected from me.

I remember when my mother was on her deathbed over twenty years ago. I was with her in the hospital, standing at her bedside when she looked up at me.

"You know what, Vickey?" she said. "I think I figured out why you're here for me. I always thought that you were a bit challenged or a weak individual, and I kept having you tested because I was sure they were going to discover there was something wrong with you, something that wasn't wired right."

This was not a surprise. Not only had my mother and I always been wired differently, but she truly was also concerned about me.

"But now," she continued, "I know that you simply march to the beat of a different drummer. You walk through life with rose-colored glasses, you always dream big, and your mind moves at the speed of lightning. And you have this gift to calm people. What I saw as a flaw was really a gift and beauty because you connect with people in a way that makes them feel worthy, and they feel as though you understand them. And you really are relatable to people from every walk of life, and you care about them.

"You believed in yourself while the rest of us did not. And you've been able to figure out and accomplish so much that I'm really, really proud of you."

It was so sweet. If I could have written the script for what my mother would say to me on her deathbed, I would have written those exact words—not that I ever would have expected her to say them, under any circumstance.

But she did. She, finally, really saw me.

• • •

A decade after my mother died, I was standing in a $50 million penthouse in New York City, waiting for a client to fly in on her private jet so I could show her the apartment. This was no ordinary penthouse—it's in the only building in Manhattan designed by Zaha Hadid, the pioneering, Pritzker Prize–winning female architect who died in 2016. It was one of her last projects.

> **If I could have written the script for what my mother would say to me on her deathbed, I would have written those exact words.**

I was standing there on the terrace looking over the High Line, taking it all in, when my phone rang. The voice on the other end said, "Hi, Vickey. This is Josh Barbanel. Do you remember me?"

Of course I remembered Josh Barbanel. He was a reporter for the *Wall Street Journal*, and pretty much everybody in the real estate business knew who he was. Besides, after the first time I met him, in a different penthouse in Manhattan, he called and asked to do a profile on me. You don't forget something like that.

Standing there on that terrace, I was flooded with feelings of appreciation for how far I'd come. It was like a wave hit me; I felt grateful, honored, and humbled, all in one moment.

Who would've thought? Who would have thought that I, little Vickey Lynn from Long Beach, California, would wind up in that penthouse—that I would be selling exclusive, high-end properties and advising celebrities, corporate leaders, and other incredibly successful people? (Although I still equally enjoy the thrill of helping a first-time buyer purchase their very first studio apartment.) It was a little surreal.

After all, I wasn't born in a Manhattan penthouse or anywhere near New York City. I entered the world in a small hospital in Baltimore, Maryland, the second daughter of a soon-to-be-single mother, who didn't even have a name for me. I'm not kidding. She was taking me out of the hospital when the nurse chased her down and said, "I'm sorry. You can't leave without a name on the birth certificate."

This was a dilemma my mother hadn't counted on. "I have no idea," she told the nurse. "I thought it was going to be a boy. Can you think of a good name for a girl?"

Who knows what she might have come up with if there hadn't been this nice woman from the South sitting in the lobby? The woman stood up and said, "Well, I think Vickey Lynn is a pretty name."

And my mother said, "Vickey Lynn. I like it. Put *Vickey Lynn* down. I gotta go."

So she brought me home, and my older sister, Diane, who was three at the time, opened the door all excited to see me and shouted, "Is that my baby brother?"

"Oh, honey, no," my mom explained. "No, we didn't have a boy. We had a girl."

To which my sister replied, "You told me I was getting a brother. I don't want a sister. Take her back."

I guess I'm lucky they decided to keep me.

When I was five, my mother decided it was too cold on the East Coast, and since my father was not in the picture, she decided to move us to the West Coast. She took Diane and me and put us on a train, and we went across the country to Southern California. She really didn't know what she was going to do when she got there, and she didn't have much money, so before long, she called my grandfather for help. His response? "Well, you're the big shot who took my grandkids all the way to California. So good luck." Then he hung up on her.

Later on, my mother told me that was the best thing that ever happened to her—because it forced her to be independent and figure things out on her own.

For a few years, we knocked around various beach towns— Manhattan (no relation) Beach, Hermosa Beach—living in motels. (Picture the motel in *Schitt's Creek*.) My mother worked tirelessly to keep a roof over our heads and food on the table. She was a very proud woman and, after her day job, would even take on side jobs, determined not to rely on others to make ends meet. And eventually, her persistence paid off. She got a job working for the aerospace firm McDonnell Douglas, and she quickly became an electrical inspector, despite the fact that she had absolutely zero experience. She went to the library to do some intensive studying, determined to pass the test, which she did. She got the job and was later promoted to manager. That's how we ended up in Long Beach.

Her example must be where my work ethic and determination come from. But beyond that, I didn't have a lot in common with my mother. It's almost like I was an alien, and somebody dropped me in our house. We'd be eating dinner, and I'd be in a deep concentration, wide-eyed, staring at my fork, and my mom would freak out.

She'd ask, "What are you doing?" thinking I was having some sort of breakdown that meant she had to get me back to the doctor to get me tested for whatever was wrong with my brain.

And I don't think my answer really helped. "No. This is not just a fork. This is a pulley. This is a handle. This could be a million different things."

My enthusiasm and vivid imagination was clear to me but concerning to my mom. My poor mom. She would look at me and shake her head. She was always shaking her head. Then she'd say, "It's a fork. Just eat your food." Plus, in case my thinking process wasn't confusing enough to my mother, I had a serious speech impediment that prevented me from speaking properly until I was six and a half years old.

So, yes, my mother and I were definitely different. However, despite those differences, she taught me self-respect, independence, and compassion toward people from all walks of life.

My mother was actually a remarkable woman, and she never really got credit for that. She had to drop out of school after the seventh grade to work to help support her family, and she got very few breaks from that day forward. Raising two kids in the '50s and '60s as a single, working mother, she still managed to keep our house immaculate, with floors so clean you could eat off of them. Eventually she was able to buy a house, then a little vacation cabin in the mountains, and later a small rental property. She worked for everything she had.

Unfortunately, it didn't exactly seem to make her happy. Even as a child, I couldn't help noticing that she was stressed out and tired and not in the greatest mood a lot of the time. She had a lot of anger and hurt in her, especially at my dad for leaving her with two little girls to raise alone—something she talked about frequently.

But it wasn't just my mom. Many of my other relatives also seemed angry. They often chose to take things personally. Even as a child, I could see that they could have just as easily ignored those slights or at least laughed them off. It was stressful—not to mention confusing! So I developed an odd way of coping that was, looking back at it, my form of meditating. When there was "static in my music," I just changed the channel in my mind. I knew in my heart that life didn't have to be so complicated.

I knew because I saw it on *Leave It to Beaver*. Like every kid in the '60s and especially every kid who had a working mom, I watched my share of TV and basically grew up with the Cleavers of *Leave It to Beaver* fame. And I couldn't help noticing that, unlike my family, the Beaver and his folks weren't always yelling and frustrated at each other. Life was always calm, nobody ever got angry, and whatever problems that did occur were wrapped up in thirty minutes flat.

They had peace.

I couldn't help wondering why my family wasn't like the Cleavers or the other families on TV or even some of my friends' families. Why did they worry so much about things that ultimately didn't matter? Or things they could not change, like their past? I found their behavior fascinating, to the point where I studied it. I watched how patterns developed and played out. I could almost predict how any individual would react in any given situation. I saw how the way they approached life influenced the choices they made and how those choices, in turn, led to very predictable outcomes. You can't plant tomatoes and expect potatoes. I learned so much about life that way, just watching people.

The things I observed over the course of my childhood taught me that things were not always going to go my way. But I also figured out, in the end, that didn't really matter. What mattered—what still matters today—is what happens next. What matters is what I call the "Now what?" It's the choice you make *after* things don't go your way that affects the outcome. Well, for me, the outcome I'm always looking for, more than anything else, is an effective harmonious solution. And I wanted to find a way to help other people achieve it too.

If anything explains how I got from Long Beach, California, to a $50 million Manhattan penthouse and a profile in *The Wall Street Journal*, I guess that's a good place to start.

CHAPTER 1

"If I Did This Job, Would I Have Fun?"

*"If you never did, you should.
These things are fun and fun is good."*

—DR. SEUSS

It was the summer after high school, and I was hanging out with my big sister, who had an interview for a job, signing local welfare recipients up for a new healthcare plan. I was waiting in the car, but it was so hot that I thought maybe I'd just head into the lobby to cool off while Diane finished up. She was the last interview of the day, so when the suit-wearing man who interviewed her walked her back into the lobby, he was puzzled to see me sitting there, a gawky eighteen-year-old with worn blue jeans and a Joni Mitchell T-shirt.

"I'm sorry," he said. "Are you here for an interview?"

I hadn't considered that possibility at all, but I didn't say, "No, I'm just waiting for my sister." Instead, I said, "It depends. First I have a question for you."

He looked puzzled. "What is that?"

"Do you happen to know how late Gemco is open?" I asked.

"Gemco?" I don't think that was the question he expected.

"Yeah," I said. "You know, the department store Gemco. Because I need to go there. I'm buying my mom a pair of slippers."

"Slippers?"

"Slippers," I explained. "You know, the fuzzy things on your feet. Do you want me to pick you up a pair?"

"No," he said with a chuckle. "I don't need any slippers. But I don't know how late they're open."

"Then I have another question," I said.

"What's that?"

"Do you mind if my sister uses the phone so we can call to find out how late Gemco is open? Because I don't want to get there and find out that it's closed."

"Okay," he said.

"Well," I said, "while she uses the phone, maybe I can sit with you? I have a couple of other questions, and then we can go from there."

He said okay, then walked me back to his office. (Note: You see how I took control of the situation, whether I knew it at the time or not.)

"I was reading the brochure," I said. "What is this FHP health plan? What exactly is my sister interviewing *for*?"

The man explained that their health plan had a contract with the state of California, and the job was to go out and enroll Medi-Cal patients, people who used the state's low-cost healthcare service, in the plan.

"So how long have you had the contract?" I asked. "And how many salespeople do this? How long have they been doing it?" And after he answered all of those questions, I said, "Describe to me the person who is the *best* person doing this job. What are they like?"

That one seemed to stump him. "I don't know," he stammered. "They're all salespeople ... there are ... different types of people—"

"I know," I interrupted. "But if you had to only keep *one* person, who is that person? Are they young? Are they old? Are they funny? Are they serious?"

He looked at me. "Well, you know ..." And he named someone he said had been doing the job and then explained that the job and the health plan were both relatively new, and in the process, he made it pretty obvious that he had no idea how to answer my question about who this hypothetical ideal salesperson might be.

So I said, "Can I ask you another question? If I did this job, would I have fun?"

That stopped him in his tracks. "Fun?"

"Oh, yeah," I said. "It's really important for me to have fun."

And he said, "Well, I don't know. No one's ever asked me that question before." And then the man in the suit grinned and said, "I have a good feeling about you."

That's how I got my first real, grown-up job—working for Dr. Robert Gumbiner, selling FHP health plans to welfare recipients—by asking him a bunch of questions. The poor man probably thought I was interviewing *him*, but, the truth is, I wasn't trying to be obnoxious or manipulative. I was curious. I asked him a lot of questions because asking questions is what I do to figure things out and get to the truth. After all, the faster we can get to the heart of the matter, the better off we all are.

It was only supposed to be a summer job, since I was planning to go to nursing school in the fall. But I never went to school to be a nurse, and I ended up working for Dr. Gumbiner for over twenty years.

My sister was hired, too, which was crucial, since I didn't have a car and she was my ride to work. Unfortunately, it quickly became clear to both of us that, while the job was a lot of things, "fun" was definitely not one of them.

The first day, they dropped us off in some neighborhood, and we had to go around knocking on doors. My sister would take one door, and I'd take the next. We'd knock, and someone would answer. That's when we'd launch into the script the company gave us that we had to follow: "Hello, my name is Vickey. I'm with the Family Health Program, and we're in the neighborhood today to see if we can—" And before I could even finish my sentence, the person would slam the door in my face or curse me out or even, on one occasion, throw something at me.

I kind of got it. It was summer, it was hot, and they were not in a good mood because they were having a hard time in life, struggling to get by. The last thing they wanted was to listen to some teenage kid reading a long, boring script, trying to get them to enroll in something that they didn't care about.

My sister was experiencing the same thing, but she reacted a little differently than I did. I'd hear her getting upset at the way the people reacted, saying "You don't have to yell at me!"

I had to calm her down. "Diane, don't. It's okay. Just go to the next door. Don't get upset by it."

We went to about fifty doors each, and, the whole time, I was puzzled. I was thinking, *This is fascinating … but this is* not *working.* So I went home that night, and I gave the job and the situation some serious thought.

The next day, when my sister and I went back out for more, Diane was already ready to quit, but I reassured her: "We're going to make it fun, and we're going to succeed."

"How are we going to make it fun?" she asked.

"Easy," I said. "We tear up the script." It was obvious to me that the script was the problem. No one wanted to take time out of their day to listen to a long spiel about a healthcare plan. Never mind my potential customers—I was putting *myself* to sleep!

So the next time I knocked on a door, I didn't wait for the person inside to open it. Instead, as I knocked, I called out, in the friendliest voice possible, "Yoo-hoo! Hello! Hi, it's me, Vickey."

A female voice from inside called back: "Vickey?"

"Yeah," I said. "Vickey. Can you come to the door? I have a quick question for you."

Me and my questions.

The woman came to the door, and I knew in that moment that I had to come up with a question that would get her to talk to me, because if I didn't, she was probably going to slam the door in my face. It was kind of a puzzle. How could I keep that from happening? How could I connect with this person so she would let me talk with her long enough to decide if the FHP health plan might actually be a good option that would make her life easier? I had no idea, but I knew whatever I said next had to be authentic. It had to be real. And then I found it.

"Oh my gosh," I exclaimed as my eyes went wide with excitement. "Is that a Siamese cat?"

"Yes," said the woman at the door.

"She has ..." I continued. "Is it a *she*?"

"Yeah, it's a *she*," replied my potential customer.

"She has the most beautiful eyes I've ever seen," I enthused. "What's her name?"

"Oh, it's Priscilla."

"Priscilla," I said. "Oh, how old is she?"

"She's two years old."

"Oh, she's beautiful, but unfortunately I'm allergic to cats, so I can't pick her up. But she sure is beautiful!"

We chatted like this for at least a minute, and the woman did not seem angry or even annoyed. She seemed comfortable with me, like a little bit of trust had been established.

Then I said, "Could you kindly go get your Medi-Cal stickers? Did you get them on time this month?"

The woman was a little confused. "My Medi-Cal stickers?"

"You know," I said, "those little stickers you get when you go to the doctor's. I need to check the number. I'm with FHP, the health

There's no better way to make a connection with another person than by asking them questions.

plan, and I need to see the number to see (a) if you're eligible for a plan that could have more convenient benefits for you and (b) if it's a good fit for you and your family."

And the woman said, "Come on in." And she let me inside, and I enrolled her in the healthcare plan.

It worked like magic.

But it wasn't really magic. It was the fact that, before I tried to sell this woman anything, I took a moment to *see* her and talk to her and connect with her as a person. That's when I first started to understand *why* the script didn't work. It wasn't just that it was boring; it was impersonal. Nobody wants to hear "what you can do for them" when you don't even know them. That's how you establish trust—by making it about the other person, not about you and how great your offer is. And there's no better way to make a connection with another person than by asking them questions.

Working for Dr. Gumbiner, I viewed every door I knocked on as another opportunity to establish a connection and make someone smile. How can I reach this person? How can I connect? I'd observe each person I met—the walls of their apartment, their kids, their pets, whatever I could grab on to—to find a way to connect and get them to open up. One time I actually said, "Do I smell chocolate chip cookies? Seriously, I love the smell of chocolate chip cookies." I took the time to reach out, to learn something about them, before I tried to pitch them anything. I'd make them laugh, and they'd smile, and they'd feel good, and their kids would like me. These were real people, with real problems, and I enjoyed my time with them.

And more often than not, they would choose to sign up for the health plan.

That, to me, was fun. Each new person had a set of challenges, and making them smile while also doing a good job and making my boss happy ... What's not to like?

I've always found joy that way: by figuring out how to solve problems as if they're puzzles. There's always a solution to a problem; you just have to find it. And to me, finding that solution is fun. And if the solution happened to be that the plan was not right for them, that was okay too.

• • •

A psychologist would probably tell me my desire to make people feel good goes back to my childhood, growing up with a mother who was overworked and stressed out. Every child wants their mother to be happy, so my mother's stress was a problem—and I desperately wanted to solve it.

One thing that was almost guaranteed to make my mother stressed was a dirty house. But because she worked, keeping things clean fell to Diane and me. And since Diane was older, she had more responsibility than I did. And since Diane was not an oddball like me, she had more friends and hated doing those chores. She would rush through, whatever tasks had been assigned so she could get outside and play with her friends. Then my mom would come home from work and immediately spot any corner that had been cut. That's when the yelling would start. Don't get me wrong; my sister keeps an immaculate house now. But as a teenager, she had an agenda—and it was not to be Molly the Maid.

Anyway, the drama over housecleaning was one of those patterns I observed—and one I really wished would go away. And then one day, I figured out how to solve that particular problem.

I would clean the house myself. I wasn't yet a teenager and clearly didn't have a full calendar.

So I decided to take action. I'd get home from school, make the bed, vacuum, clean the kitchen—and then I kept going. I looked around the house and figured out what needed to be moved, polished, scrubbed, or rearranged. Wouldn't it be fun to make our house look like the Cleaver house or a house in a magazine? I didn't mind being Molly—I straightened every corner and made every inch of our house look perfect. And when she walked in, instead of yelling, my mother said, "Oh my! This is amazing!" She was happy. There was no yelling. There was peace.

It felt great.

Eventually I figured out that if it worked at home, it would work in other places too—like at my best friend Cecilia's house. Her mother (also a single mother with a bit of stress) would say, "You have to vacuum the living room! You're lazy!"

And she'd say, "I'm lazy? You're the mother, and you can't even keep your house clean. You're making your twelve-year-old do it? And what about my brothers? Can't they help?" And the fighting would start.

I would whisper to Cecilia, "It's okay. Let's just do it. Let's get it done." So we vacuumed for her. And—just like at my house—the yelling stopped, and there was peace. And, even better, we could go outside and play. (Note: Always remember you have the choice to take control of a situation and change the outcome.)

When I started working for other people and getting paid to do it, I approached every job the same way. When I would babysit, after I put the kids to bed, instead of watching TV, I would wash the dishes, clean the counters, sweep the floors, vacuum, even fluff the throw pillows on the couch. I would be so excited for the parents to walk in, see their house, and smile. There is value in going the extra mile.

• • •

At fourteen, I got my first real job at—where else?—McDonald's. One time when it was slow, I dragged this giant ladder out of the back to clean the dust balls off a fan that looked like it hadn't been touched in years. I was up there, cleaning away, when my manager walked in and said, "Vickey, what are you doing?"

And I said, "I'm getting the dust balls off the fan."

He said, "But that's not your job!"

I replied, "Whose job is it?" And we both laughed.

My manager was pretty surprised. I remember him saying, "Who cleans a dusty fan for fun?"

Me, I guess. I get a feeling of satisfaction putting things in order and making a place shine, whether it's a McDonald's in Long Beach or a townhouse in New York City. But even beyond making my June Cleaver side happy, I love the reaction. I love those little moments when I see someone's face light up. Getting paid on top of that is just the icing on the cake.

That's my idea of fun.

It wasn't, however, my sister's. She didn't see any possibility of fun hiding under all the rejection and anger she encountered selling FHP health plans. And after about three weeks, she couldn't take it anymore. She quit the job—and she wasn't the only one! I would soon learn that there was typically a revolving door of salespeople.

Honestly, I don't blame any of them. Most people don't like rejection, let alone being yelled at!

Dr. McCauley, a doctor who I hired at a later stage of my career (we'll get to that soon) came to visit my home this summer, and we were reminiscing about jobs we had in our youth. When I told him that I worked at this particular job for eight years, his mouth dropped open. He shared that he, too, had a job that was very much like that—and he only lasted four days! He told me he could remember vividly how petrified he was each time he knocked on a door, cringing and praying nobody would open it. He was sure that he was going to get rejected and whoever opened the door would not buy anything.

Ironically, he is now a very successful doctor and entrepreneur, with forty-plus clinics. Clearly he figured out how to strengthen his strengths, not his weaknesses—and you should too. But we'll get to that in a bit.

The only problem with Diane quitting was that she was also my ride to work. I had to go to the man in the suit and tell him, "My sister quit, so I have to quit because I don't have a car, and my Huffy bike is not going to cut it." But the man in the suit didn't want me to quit. It turned out I was signing up more people for health plans than anyone else on their staff—*ever*.

So he said, "If we find someone that can pick you up every day and bring you to work, will you not quit?"

I thought, *Who's going to want to do that?* But a woman volunteered to pick me up and bring me in, and I ended up being their number one salesperson. My numbers were off the chart. I would enroll 210 people, and the next salesperson would enroll 67.

At some point, the manager of our office went on vacation, and, knowing I was an early riser, he asked if I'd open up while he was away. I saw an opportunity to share some of what was working for me with my coworkers. I basically assumed the manager's role. No one asked me to; I just did it. Each morning, I started checking everyone in with a little pep talk: "All right, you guys, go on out there! Remember: have fun and be nice to people and don't get angry if they're angry. Just remember they might not be having a good day. Remember to be above that, and just be really kind. And have fun!" Fun was so important; I had to mention it twice. "I'll meet you back here at four o'clock."

It must have made an impact, because pretty soon the man in the suit called me back into his office and said, "We want to promote you to be a manager."

"A manager?" I said. "That doesn't sound like a fun job. That sounds serious."

I was only eighteen at the time, and it did sound like an awful lot of responsibility.

But the man in the suit was insistent. "No, Vickey. You have a skill. You have been selling more than anybody, and you've been running the office while the manager's on vacation—and you've been doing so well we want to promote you to *be* the manager and keep selling!" He couldn't believe I was so hesitant. Who wouldn't want a better title and more money after only a couple of months?

Well ... me. I wasn't trying to get promoted—I was just trying to focus on my job, on each individual person behind each door I knocked on. I was having fun and making money and well on my way to my goal of saving enough money to buy a car. I was not interested in changing things up.

But the man in the suit would not give up. "You can do it," he said. "You've been doing the whole thing anyway. All you have to do is come get everyone's checks on Friday."

He wanted me to be a manager so badly ... and he made it sound so simple ... and I was already doing the job anyway. How could I say no? So I bought a car (a blue 1967 Toyota), and I got a little briefcase. My first Friday as manager, I went and picked up the first packet of checks, put them all in my briefcase, like the grown-up, professional manager that I was, and—

And I left the briefcase in the restroom.

Seriously? I was horrified. This was the biggest mistake I had ever made in my short career, and I was sure the man in the suit was going to fire me for failing as a manager, just as I predicted I would.

I went to a pay phone (this was long before cell phones) and called up my boss and said, "See? You should *not* have promoted me. I already left all the checks in the bathroom."

But the man in the suit didn't care that I left my briefcase full of checks in the restroom. Instead, he said, very calmly, "Just come back and get the checks. We have them here."

So I got the checks and learned a valuable lesson in the process: you can mess up and people will forgive you, as long as they know your heart (and your attitude) is in the right place.

Eventually, I got promoted again, this time to a job where I was interviewing and hiring the salespeople. I trained them to sell the way I did, without a script and with a lot of questions and a lot of empathy. It's all about discovery and the process. I tried to teach them not to take rejection personally or to get upset when people got angry. I showed them that selling was really about helping people solve their problems, and in order to do that, they needed to take the time to get a sense of who each potential customer was and what they were going through. The goal was to find a way to connect with them and establish trust *before* trying to sell them a healthcare plan. And because sometimes whatever you are trying to sell somebody might not be a good fit, I told them that was okay, too, and that they should just accept the results and move on. Their energy should move to "Now what?"—because that's what really matters.

That's how it works in any business, and even in life.

CHAPTER 2

"Is the Tile on Sale Today or Saturday?"

"Everything is negotiable. Whether or not the negotiation is easy is another thing."

—CARRIE FISHER

At the age of twenty, after two years at FHP, I decided to buy a home of my own. I didn't have that much money saved, but I didn't see the point of paying rent when that money could be going into my own home.

I drove around and saw a For Sale by Owner sign in a townhouse development, near where I lived, called Tanglewood. I walked up, knocked on the door, and said, "Hi. It's me, Vickey. Can I come and look at your house?" The man who answered the door said yes.

I looked around. It was a two-bedroom, one-bathroom, just over eight hundred square feet. It was cute. I liked it. I went back to the man and his wife, who was with him inside the townhouse, and said, "I have a question for you. I like this house. I can really see myself living here. So can you do me a favor and allow me two days? I'm going to go to Bank of America right now and see if they can give me a mortgage, and then I can buy your house—and it's going to be good."

They were so sweet. They said, "Sure. Just go to the bank."

It sounded too easy. So I said, "Can we have a code of honor? I'll sign something now, and I'll give you some sort of earnest deposit, but don't sell it to anyone else until you give me time to see if the bank will lend me the money."

They said, "Don't worry. You have our word. You go to the bank."

So I drove to the bank, and I walked in. I was barely twenty years old—I was a child! I remember going up to the counter, saying, "Hi. I found a house that I'm buying, and I need to talk to a mortgage officer to get my mortgage." (Note: Don't position yourself to get an answer you don't want. There is power in your words. Notice I did not say a "house I want to buy" and "if I can get a mortgage"—there is a big difference.)

I sat in front of this woman, with big hair and bright-red lipstick, and filled out applications. I didn't know anything about houses or mortgages—but I got a mortgage, and I bought that house.

That was my first experience with real estate.

The house was cute, but it wasn't *that* cute. And my June Cleaver fantasy required a house that was really cute. So I decided I would fix the place up, beginning with the tile, which was one of the not cute things that bothered me. I went to the tile store and walked in and said, "I just bought a house, and I need to buy some tile."

The tile guy showed me some gray tile, and I checked the price. It was more than I could afford, but I really wanted that tile. So I did something that most people would probably think is a little crazy. I asked the tile guy when the sale for the tile—which was not on sale—started.

He replied, as you might expect, "What?"

I repeated, "Is the tile on sale today, Tuesday? Or do I have to wait for Saturday for the sale?"

"What sale?"

"The sale for the tile."

"Well, let me go talk to … I don't know that the tile is on sale."

"I think it's coming on sale. I just don't know what day that is."

So he walked back to get the manager, and the manager came back and said, "No, the tile's not on sale."

This is where one might stop. But I really wanted that tile, and I really didn't want to pay the price they were asking. In fact, if I had to pay that price, I really couldn't afford the tile. So I decided to take a chance.

I said, "Don't you think it's a really good idea to put that tile on sale?" The worst thing they could say was no, right?

Instead, the tile guy and the manager both smiled, which I took as an encouraging sign.

So I opened up to them and said, "I just bought my first house. I don't even know how Bank of America gave me a mortgage, but they did. I don't think they saw the tile. It's not very cute, and I need this tile right here. I just need you to sharpen the pencil a little bit and get me a better price."

The manager said, "Well, we don't really do that."

Again, most people would have given up. They said no. Twice! But then again, I had nothing to lose. It wasn't like they were going to kick me out of the store or throw a tile at my head. Worst case scenario: I just wouldn't be able to buy the tile I wanted. But if I kept trying, there was still a chance I would get it, and at a price I could afford.

So I said, "That answer makes me sad. Maybe, just maybe, you'll give me good news."

The manager looked at me and smiled and said, "We'll give you the designer discount of 20 percent off."

I said, "I like that answer." And I bought the tile. (Note: Notice I never questioned their pricing or threatened that I could get it down the street for less money. I chose to empower them, positioning them to be the hero and get to the finish line.)

The only reason I got what I wanted was because I made it happen. I asked for what I wanted, and since I knew I had nothing to lose, I wasn't afraid to keep asking, even after the tile guy and his manager told me no, even if I was maybe being a little annoying.

I redid the tile on my new house, put new carpet in, painted, and wallpapered the bathroom, and after ten months, I sold it for

The only reason I got what I wanted was because I made it happen.

$79,000. I bought it for $57,000, which meant I made a nice profit by flipping my first house—several decades before flipping was even a thing. That was my introduction into real estate. Okay, I was my only client. I still had my career with Dr. Gumbiner, which went on for a long time (more on that later). But while I worked for him, I kept buying houses, fixing them up, keeping them for a year or two, then selling them and doing it again. I loved it.

I had bought and sold three more houses when I found the house in Fullerton. That house was beautiful. It was my ultimate June Cleaver fantasy come to life, with five bedrooms and a pool and a cabana in the back. It was also listed above my price point. But I wanted that house.

I walked through it when the owner, an older man named Dr. Sears, was at home. I said, "I love this house." He could see how much I loved it. But then I left. After all, there was no way I could afford the house. But I kept thinking about it, dreaming big. I really wanted that house. There had to be a way to solve the problem of not being able to afford it.

So I came up with a plan. I called my broker, Mark Burrell, to tell him about it. "Could you call and get a meeting with that nice Dr. Sears?" I asked. "I know I shouldn't be buying a house at this price point, but I can't stop thinking about his house. So my idea is that maybe we could own the home together, but I'll live in it? I'm really good at fixing places up, so I'll redo it, and we'll agree that I'll sell it in two or three years, and then we'll split the profit. Will you call him and tell him that I said that?"

He said, "Well, no one's ever done that."

I said, "I'm telling you: this is going to work." Mark trusted me and certainly knew me; this was our fourth transaction in four years together. So I said, "You call that man. I remember he related to me. And he's going to want to help me. And I think he's going to do this."

Mark called the owner, and the owner said he was excited to meet with me. So we sat down and laid out my plan for him. He said, "Well, I'm a little old." He was in his sixties, a doctor in linguistics. "At this age I am not sure I am interested in that venture."

In other words, he said no. And I could have let it go. I could have given up. But again, I wanted to buy that house. He wanted to sell that house. *What did I have to lose?*

So instead of thanking him for his time and leaving, I was honest with him about how I felt. I told him, "That is not the answer I wanted. And it makes me just a little bit sad to hear you say that, to be honest. So can you come up with a better plan of how I can live in this house? Because I love this house."

He said, "I'll tell you what I'll do." Interest rates, by the way, were over 14 percent at the time. "How much can you afford a month?"

I said, "I'm pretty conservative, and I'm not reckless with my money. You promise not to laugh?"

"I won't laugh."

So I told him my budget.

He took out his pencil and did some calculations. Then he said, "Okay, I'll tell you what I'll do. I will carry the whole mortgage for the home. Are you sure that budget is not a stretch for you?"

"No, I can afford it. I've always been good with budgeting my money. I've been a saver my whole life."

"Okay. So that means the interest rate will be 3 percent."

He carried the mortgage for that house, at 3 percent simple interest, for thirty years. And it never would have happened if I had given up. (Note: Make things happen; don't wait for them to happen.)

Unbelievable. Who does that?

Honestly, the answer is more people than you think. I know Dr. Sears was a gift from somewhere, and I am so grateful. But I never would have gotten that gift if I hadn't been willing not only to ask for what I wanted and to look for a solution but also to keep going when that solution didn't work for me—giving *him* an opportunity to find one that worked for himself. He became the hero, and we wound up with a win-win situation—just like with the tile guy.

The reality is that sometimes people want to make your day. Sometimes they want to give you a break. Sometimes they're ready to make a sale, even at a lower price than they're asking for. You just have to give them the opportunity.

I know this is easier for me than it is for a lot of people. I don't know why rejection doesn't bother me. But it's not that it doesn't; it's just that I put it in perspective. I know the word "no" isn't the end of the world. I know it isn't personal. Hey, sometimes *I* have to say no!

But I also know saying yes is much more fun. And getting people to say yes—getting them to want to be a part of making somebody happy—is another thing I think is fun.

• • •

Maybe because I have spent so much time observing patterns of behavior, I tend to see the end before the beginning. And I am a believer in people. I truly believe that, underneath it all, most people want to help others. Giving them a chance to do that is all about asking the right question and then presenting them with the opportunity. When you enlist other people's help and welcome them into assisting you across the finish line, you also give them the opportunity to feel good about helping you get there.

My friend Gayle calls this "that thing you do."

I've known Gayle for over forty years, and she is involved in a charity I admire and support (more on that later). And recently, she had her eye on this big armoire. This armoire was listed for $14,000, and she wanted a discount in the worst way. So she called me up in New York and said, "Vickey, I tried to do what you do, and it's not working. The man is not budging. He will not give me one dollar off the stupid armoire. I really, really want a discount. Will you please just call and do that thing you do?"

I said, "Gayle, I'm really busy—"

"I'm begging you. I really want that armoire."

So I asked her, "What's his name?"

"George."

So I called George. "George, it's me, Vickey. I have a question for you."

George said, "What?"

"Is it true you sell the most unique armoires in LA?"

And he responded, "Yes, I have about four of them in my showroom now."

"Perfect. My friend went in and saw one priced at $14,000. Is that still available?"

"Yes," he said.

"Amazing. Now here is where I need your help, George. You met my friend, Gayle, and she really wants that armoire, but it's a little bit above her budget."

"We don't give discounts," George said.

"I get it. With the most unique armoires in LA, I probably would not discount either. Maybe pretend she's a famous interior designer, and giver her a discount. Or maybe she was the thousandth person through your showroom and won a big fat coupon. Something creative."

He told me to give him a minute, and he put me on hold.

When he came back, he said, "I'll tell you what I'll do. I'll give her a trade discount of 20 percent for $11,200, but she'll have to pay for delivery and have it out by Friday because I have another piece coming in."

"Sold! George, thank you. That was generous and much appreciated. And just so you know, Gayle is a very generous, giving individual. She helps so many people all of the time, so you could not have helped a better person."

Gayle got her discount, and I got to keep my sanity. And so did George. At this point, you might be thinking, *I could never do that.* But you *can.* I promise. It's all about observing people and empowering them. In this case, I got George to think about how often Gayle was calling him asking for a discount and then the prospect of those calls continuing about just one armoire; ultimately, he decided that selling the armoire for a smaller profit was worth it if it meant the calls would stop. Every problem has a unique solution, so it all comes down to asking the right questions to get the person to open up so you can figure out how to give them something they want—or, at the very least, a laugh and a good story. (Note: Remember to always thank the hero [in this case, George] for making it happen.)

CHAPTER 3

"Are You Picking Contestants for the Show Right Now?"

"You create your opportunities by asking for them."

—SHAKTI GAWAIN

It was May 1975, and my mother had received tickets for the TV game show *The Price Is Right*. Well, it turned out my mom couldn't go, so she sent me, and off I went to Burbank. I had to wait in a long line before they would let us in to sit in the audience, and I was wondering exactly how long I was going to have to stand there, when I spotted this man in a plaid shirt walking with a young lady with a clipboard. I knew right then he was picking the people who were going to be called to "Come on down!" from the audience to be on the show. And I wanted very much to be one of them.

I was so excited. I started pacing back and forth. I must have looked like a crazy person or someone with a full bladder. Nobody else in line was pacing, just me. But sure enough, when the man in the plaid shirt got to me, he stopped. I guess he couldn't help but notice my energy and enthusiasm (and pacing).

He looked at my name tag and said, "Hello, Vickey." And I just knew this was my moment.

I looked around, confused. All of the other people in line were just standing around looking melancholy. Did they not understand what was about to happen? *I* did, which was why I immediately answered, "Hello, sir. May I ask you a quick question?"

He nodded yes.

And I said, "That person with the clipboard next to you," gesturing at the woman who was walking with him, "is she writing the names of the people you are selecting to be on the show? Because, in my heart of hearts, I kind of think that is what is happening right now. Am I right?"

He said I was.

"I knew it!" I said, with more than a little excitement.

"Why are you so excited?" he asked.

"Because I see myself on the show winning prizes!"

The man looked at me. "How do you know you're going to be on the show?

"Well," I said, "there is no reason you should *not* pick me."

He smiled at me. "Why is that?"

"Well," I replied, thoughtfully, "(a) I'm of age,"—I was eighteen—"(b) I need a lot of things, and (c) I love winning prizes."

Then the man asked, "Oh, do you know Stanley?" Stanley was the tall man standing next to me.

I said, "Do you want me to know Stanley?"

He nodded.

So I turned to the man next to me and said, "Hello, Stanley. I'm Vickey. Nice to meet you." I then turned back to the man in the plaid shirt and said, "Pick Stanley too. He seems nice."

The man in the plaid shirt and the woman with the clipboard moved on. The line finally moved, too, and we got to go inside and sit down and watch the show. Not long after, the announcer called my name. I heard "Vickey—" and, before he could get my last name out, ran down saying, "I knew it! I knew it! I knew it!" Thank goodness I was the right "Vickey." He could have been calling "Vickey Matthews." How embarrassing would that have been? But it *was* me, and there I was on *The Price Is Right*!

It turned out I was really good at figuring out how much things cost. (No wonder pricing turned out to be one of my favorite things about real estate.) We had to price a kitchen range, and my number was closer than the other three contestants', which meant I got to go on the big stage and play the "real" game. I got to play Race Game, where you run around with price tags and match them to different items. I got the most amount right that I wound up the top winner of the day and got to the play at the end of the show for the ultimate prize: the showcase. (This was before they had the big wheel.) I got to go first and decide if I wanted to bid on the first showcase or pass it to the other contestant.

The first showcase was amazing. There was a trip to Switzerland. There was also a Jeep, which definitely would have come in handy, since my blue 1967 Toyota was cute but *old*. But the package also included rock-climbing equipment, and I didn't know anything about rock climbing. So how could I possibly figure out what that would cost? So I told Bob Barker, as much as I wanted to go to Switzerland and drive that Jeep, I had to pass and let the other contestant bid on it.

The next showcase—*my* showcase—was not quite as glamorous. There was a fireplace; a stereo in a cabinet (it was 1975, and that was a thing then); a Pfaff sewing machine (which my daughter Teka still sews on); twelve cans of Pam; and, as a bonus, a brand-new AMC Gremlin. Turned out I hadn't given up my shot at a new car after all!

Once I'd seen all the goodies, it was my turn to bid on what I thought the whole package was worth. Now, if you've never seen *The Price Is Right* (which I acknowledge is possible but not likely), I should explain that the trick is to get as close as possible to the retail price of whatever you're pricing *without going over*, or you lose automatically.

I trusted my gut, and my gut said my price was right. And it was.

That was my challenge. I had to come up with a number that was *slightly* less than what all that stuff was worth, but only slightly.

I looked at everything, worked through it all in my mind, did the math, and came up with a number that seemed reasonable. I blurted my number into the microphone. And the audience started booing me!

Bob Barker looked at me. He said, very gently and kindly, "Vickey, everyone thinks your price is too high. It's not too late. Would you like to adjust your price?"

I took my index finger, and I tapped my front tooth. All the people out in the audience thought I was wrong. Bob Barker seemed to think I was wrong. But when I went through all the numbers in my mind, I just couldn't get to that place where *I* felt like I was wrong. So I said, "You know what, Bob? I kind of like my number. I'm sticking with it."

The boos got louder, but I trusted my gut.

And guess what? My price was closer, which meant I won my showcase and the game. In fact, I came so close to the price of my showcase (without going over) that I almost won *both* showcases! If you're within $100, you get both. But I was $175 off—$75 closer and I would have won two cars and a trip to Switzerland and probably double the number of cans of Pam.

So, of course, I hurried home (still in my blue 1967 Toyota since I couldn't just leave it there!) and called my mom to share the news that I'd won.

She flat out did not believe me.

She was a little upset and distracted at the time because the Avon lady had died, so she handed the phone to my sister, saying, "You talk to her. I am too upset for her humor and pranks." Luckily, my sister believed me and was able to convince my mother that I actually won. My mother grabbed the phone back and said, "Vickey Lynn, you little shit. You are the luckiest person I know."

She was right. I definitely did get lucky that day. What if my mom had gone to see the show instead of me? What if the other showcase had something else in it that I knew nothing about, like a welding set?

But I never would have been chosen to be on the show, and had the opportunity to play the game instead of just watching it, if I hadn't made it happen by engaging the man in the plaid shirt and getting him to talk to me. If I hadn't, I'm 99.99 percent sure someone else would have gone home with all those cans of Pam that day.

And I also wouldn't have taken home the Pam and all the other goodies if I had listened to, well, everyone. I trusted my gut, and my gut said *my* price was right. And it was.

Both of the things I did that put the Gremlin in my garage and the Pam in my pantry fall under the heading of "Making Your Own Luck." The seemingly magical things that happen don't just *happen*; we make them come about by looking for opportunities and grabbing them when we see them. (And for me, it's not being afraid of looking silly in order to do it.)

By the way, my mother got the stereo in the cabinet.

• • •

Another time I got really lucky was when I drove over two hours in the snow to the Amish country with my colleague Mary on a business trip. Mary had decided she wanted to pick up a genuine Amish quilt, even though the Amish country was a long drive from where we were. But she wanted the quilt, so off we went. Who doesn't love an adventure? The problem was that it was the dead of winter, and by the time we got there, it was dark, and everything was closed. We appeared to be … well, *out* of luck.

But as we were driving around, I suddenly spotted a house with a lantern in a window. I turned to Mary and said, "I'm getting you a quilt. We didn't drive here for over two hours for you not to get a quilt."

Mary said, "Vickey, what are you talking about? This isn't a store; it's a house. How are you going to get a quilt?"

I said, "They are going to have a quilt."

I got out of the car, and I knocked on the door. A little girl came, with her prayer hat.

I said, "Hi. It's me, Vickey. This is my friend, Mary. We drove a long way, and my friend's kind of looking for a quilt. Do you happen to know where we can get a quilt?"

The little girl called out, "Mama!"

Her mother came to the door. She said, "Can I help you?"

I started explaining our quilt dilemma. While looking through the door, I spotted a hand-carved rocker, and so I asked the woman, "Is that a hand-carved rocker?"

"Yes. We make them. Would you like to come in?"

It turned out that downstairs, in that very house, they had someone making lots of quilts to sell. So Mary got her quilt.

I said, "What about that rocking chair? I'd love to buy that rocking chair." Then I bought the prayer hat off the girl's head ... and the mother's prayer hat ... and the kitchen rug from the grandmother's house next door. I saw it and said, "That is the cutest little rug. Can I buy that rug?" I bought one of the blankets they use for the horses that pull the carriages. We wound up shopping in their house for about two hours. I would have bought the front door, but I didn't know how to get it home.

Was I lucky that the door I happened to knock on also happened to belong to a lovely family of Amish artisans with a houseful of stuff just waiting to be sold? Of course I was! Even though it was nothing earth shattering, it was definitely one of those movie moments. What were the odds?

But then again, how many people would have knocked on that door in the first place?

That's what I mean by making your own luck. It can mean stepping outside your comfort zone and taking a chance. Remember: the worst thing is you'll get a "no," which means you really have nothing to lose.

I'm not saying it's always that easy. Sometimes a "no" is a "hard no" (which means "absolutely, definitely no"), in which case you have to move on. But at other times, magically turning that "no" into a "yes" is just a matter of being inquisitive, persistent, and maybe a little creative. In real estate and in life, you are a market maker or an order taker.

• • •

Recently, I was trying to get a reservation at this restaurant in Manhattan. I called them up and asked if they had a table for five on Saturday night, and the receptionist said they were totally booked, which is completely normal for a restaurant on a Saturday night in Manhattan.

But I happen to know that it's also common for Manhattan restaurants to hold a table or two back in case a VIP shows up unannounced—like, if Oprah suddenly appeared in the doorway and needed a table for five, they're not going to turn her away or send her and Stedman to the bar to wait. So I kept going and asked the receptionist if she meant "*Booked* booked."

And the receptionist confirmed that, yes, they were *booked* booked.

I said, "Darn it."

But I wasn't quite ready to give up. I really wanted to eat in this particular restaurant. So I asked the hostess if I could ask her a question, and she said I could.

"Is that chef cooking those really good lamb chops on Saturday?"

"Yes," she said. "The lamb chops will be on the menu on Saturday."

"Oh! That's really what I'm talking about! I really want those lamb chops. So can I ask you another question?"

The receptionist said okay again.

"What are the chances that someone might cancel?"

"It's possible," she said, "but unlikely."

"Well," I said, "can we just focus on the word *possible* for one second? Because I liked the sound of the possible part because that gives me hope, and I really, really want those lamb chops. So do I need permission? Can I call back? I don't want to bother you, but I kind of want to just keep calling back. 'Cause in my heart of hearts, I kind of think someone's going to maybe be watching their favorite series, and they're going to get glued to the TV and then forget about the time and call and cancel. Or, you know, the flu's going around. That can happen, for sure. Something's going to happen. I think I'm eating those lamb chops, and I'm calling you back."

So a while later, I called back and said, "Hi, it's me, the lamb chop lady. Has anyone called in with the flu, or are they watching TV?"

And the woman said, "No, not yet."

I said, "Okay. Please don't hate me if I call back. I know how busy you are and how hard you are working." And guess what? When I called back again, the receptionist said, "We've got a table for you." And I thanked her and told her she was a rock star.

You might be thinking, *Aha! You got lucky!* And yes, I did; *however*, I don't think it happened because a table suddenly, magically opened up. I don't think anyone came down with the flu or forgot to stop watching their favorite series. I think the woman at the restaurant just didn't know what to do with me. She almost *had* to find a table for me, because I was no longer just another whiner begging for a table at a New York City restaurant on a Saturday night. (That's the persistent part. But by itself, persistence can get kind of annoying, right?)

I think the reason I got that table is that I combined persistence with creativity and a human connection. I made myself into someone unforgettable—the lamb chop lady! I not only gave the receptionist a story but made her a character in that story. *Will the lamb chop lady get her lamb chops? Or will the receptionist cruelly and callously crush her dream on the off-off-off chance Oprah Winfrey shows up?*

Maybe I was a little annoying, but it was a *fun* kind of annoying. It was the kind of annoying you go home and tell your husband or roommate or best friend about. And that—plus the fact that I was always nice, polite, and understanding of her position—was enough to get that receptionist on my side or, at least, to make her decide that she needed to get me to stop calling.

Sometimes, getting lucky just means not giving up until somebody says yes. And that doesn't take any magical powers at all.

CHAPTER 4

"Can You Guess What I Do for a Living?"

"You can't get what you want
till you know what you want."

—JOE JACKSON

My boss, Dr. Gumbiner, was continuing to expand his business. That's how I met my friend Gary. He was considering a sales position at FHP, and they said, "Oh, you should meet Vickey because she's the top salesperson." He asked if he could hang out with me and watch me do my thing.

I said, "Sure," and so he came out with me for a few days. He turned out to be an oddball like me, and his goal was to have fun! We were great together, and he took the job.

After a while, Gary and I figured out that, instead of knocking on doors, we could save a lot of time and sign a lot more people up by going to the welfare office and hanging out there. So we did that for a while with tremendous results, and then Dr. Gumbiner told us that he was adding a senior citizen plan, to work with Medicare.

I have kind of an interesting history with senior citizens. When I was eight, I really wanted to play the piano. Then one day, after I came home from a friend's house, my mother said, "Vickey Lynn, guess what? I know you wanted a piano, but I got you an accordion! It is kind of like a piano. It has keys on the side!"

I thought to myself, *You must be kidding*, but I saw the happiness on my mother's face, and that touched my heart. She didn't have the money, so she put the accordion on a payment plan. I said, "Wow, this is beautiful! And the good news is I can take it with me places!" And that's exactly what I did.

I got ten free lessons with the purchase, so I learned to play polkas, which made my mom happy because we are Eastern European. I'd play for all her friends and at family gatherings, and she even had me go to Serbian picnics and play. Then she had the great idea that I could use my music to make people at the senior center happy.

My mother had a big heart and taught us to give to others in need, and she told us that, sometimes, the people at the senior center were lonely. So we'd wrap up small gifts, like books, lotions, and socks, and take them to the senior center. My mother would ask the nurses to gather everyone and meet in the recreation hall. We'd pass out the gifts, and I would play my accordion and polka my heart out. Was I good at it? Not especially. But I had fun, and it made me so happy to see the them smile—and to see my mother smile.

I don't know if that early experience with the elderly was why I did so well signing up seniors for Dr. Gumbiner's new health plan. The plan grew and grew, and then my best friend, Cecelia, also joined the division to help, and she was instrumental in the success of the plan. Soon, we had an entirely new problem: we enrolled so many people in such a short period that we didn't have enough doctors to take care of them all. So Dr. Gumbiner called Gary and me into his office and said, "I need two volunteers, and the two of you are my choice"—which, looking back, doesn't sound exactly like volunteering, although it's not like I would have said no.

Instead, I asked, "To do what?"

Dr. Gumbiner said, "You need to go shake the bushes and find some quality doctors."

Shake the bushes for doctors? No one had ever done that before. But we had, indeed, enrolled so many seniors that we didn't have enough doctors to take care of them. We left the meeting, and I thought, *Okay, we have to figure this out and fast.*

Three weeks went by, then Dr. Gumbiner called me back into his office to ask about my progress finding doctors. He asked, "Can you tell me how it's going and what progress you've made?"

I said, "Okay. But can I tell you a secret?"

His eyes went wide as he said, "What?"

"I don't have a clue what I'm doing."

"Perfect."

"You like that I don't know what I'm doing?"

"Yes, because you don't know that it can't be done. With your creativity, I'm confident you are going to figure it out."

I was touched. Dr. Gumbiner had so much faith in me. And, because he did, that inspired me to work even harder.

"So you want me to tell you what we've done so far?" I asked.

He said he did.

"Well, you told me you needed internists. So I thought, *Where can we find internists? Aha! The VA hospital.*"

He said, "The VA hospital? Good thinking. So what'd you do?"

"Well," I said, "I just hung out in the cafeteria."

"The cafeteria? What'd you do in there?"

"Well, for starters, I ate a lot. It was really easy to figure out who the doctors were, so I would get my tray and just park myself next to them."

"And then what would you do?" he asked.

"Then I'd just ask them a question."

Of course he wanted to know what this magic question was.

I'd say, "So I obviously know what you do for a living, but I bet you don't know what I do for a living." And then they would smile, and I'd say, "Seriously. Try to guess what I do for a living." And they would say a schoolteacher or an artist, or they'd come up with something else that sounded reasonable.

That's when I'd say, "I'm a physician recruiter. So, see, we have something in common: you're a doctor, and I'm a doctor finder—and here we are. I have another question for you. Have you ever heard of FHP, the health plan? Did you know that the state contracted with us to take care of senior citizens? We enrolled so many that we are now in need of additional doctors to take care of them. Would you be available either Tuesday or Thursday so I can introduce you to Dr. Gumbiner and he can share his vision for healthcare with you?"

I got three interviews like that—just from hanging out in the cafeteria, looking for people to talk to, and then, of course, asking them questions.

But waiting in the cafeteria took time, and three interviews wasn't a lot. I needed a solution that would help me reach more doctors faster, and I realized that the key was getting to the administration person who hired all the residents. If I could get to the residents who were about to graduate, I could recruit them to come work for Dr. Gumbiner right away. So I convinced an ER doctor, Dr. Realmuto, who just started at FHP, to join me in giving presentations to the residents. We were a successful duo and still laugh about it to this day.

When I would present, I used a lot of the same strategy I used when I dealt with people one on one. I would just ask a question like "So you're here, you're in your specialty. You chose internal medicine. How many of you contemplated playing in a rock band instead?" Just like I did when I went door to door selling health plans to Medi-Cal patients, I always started by asking authentic questions from my own curiosity, just to get them to relax and feel comfortable

It's all about the human connection, and to succeed, you must discover who they are.

with me and connect with me. It's all about the human connection, and to succeed, you must discover who they are. *Then* I'd ask whether they'd be interested in coming to work for Dr. Gumbiner and helping seniors and launching their medical careers.

It worked out really well, and soon Dr. Gumbiner had all the internists he needed.

He was so impressed with my accomplishments that he decided I should have a new office. In fact, he decided I should have *his* office, which was up on a high floor in this beautiful high-rise building on Ocean Boulevard in Long Beach. He brought me in and smiled and announced, "Here's your new office."

My new office? It was enormous. Seriously, you could have landed a plane in there. I said, "It's too big, and it scares me. What am I supposed to do in here?" I felt like Tom Hanks in that movie *Big*—like any minute they would realize that I was just this little kid and had no idea what I was doing.

But Dr. Gumbiner insisted. So I took the office, but I moved Gary in with me. And we shared the office, partners in crime, and that was really, really fun.

After that, Dr. Gumbiner expanded his practice again, this time opening a new clinic with offices in Micronesia—on the islands of Saipan and Guam. We're talking about medical clinics basically halfway around the world, in the middle of the Pacific Ocean. And once again, Dr. Gumbiner wanted me to find and recruit doctors to work at the clinic.

This was not going to be an easy task. I had never stepped foot on either Guam or Saipan. How was I going to get doctors to uproot their entire lives and move thousands of miles from home? When I asked Dr. Gumbiner that question, he smiled and said, "I trust you'll figure it out." So I realized I needed to understand what type of doctors would be happy working on an island in the middle of the ocean. I did my homework, asked a million questions, and got an understanding of the culture and the lay of the land. So I knew exactly (or as close to exactly as I could) what I was asking these doctors to do.

Getting a doctor to leave their practice, leave their home, leave their friends and family, and fly to the middle of nowhere for an assignment on an island, site unseen, and commit to the position for two years—well, you can see why I had to build a level of trust. But being a doctor on a tropical island had to be a dream job for someone, right? I just needed to figure out what kind of questions to ask to get the information necessary to determine who was right for the job—and to help them decide if the job was right for them.

And in order to do that—and match people who were really ready for this kind of adventure—I had to be honest about everything that adventure would entail.

When you think of a successful salesperson, you probably picture one of those hard-charging people who never take no for an answer and can sell underwear to a nudist. That's one reason people are uncomfortable with sales. They look at it as getting somebody—even if that means tricking somebody—to do something they don't really want to do.

I don't do that.

Obviously, the fact that I'm one of the top real estate agents in Manhattan means I've sold a lot of underwear to a lot of nudists. The difference is that I'll only sell underwear to a nudist if that nudist actually needs the underwear. And, of course, I'll ask a lot of questions to find out why they need it—and what kind of underwear, what they intend to do with it, how many pairs of underwear they're looking for, and a host of other underwear-related details I won't bore you with here.

The point is this: selling doesn't have to be about making somebody do something. For me, it's about helping somebody discover what they really want and then helping them get it. It's kind of like being a fairy godmother; it's about making people's dreams come true. And how amazing is that!

Of course, to be able to make people's dreams come true, you have to know what those dreams actually are. That's trickier than it might sound. That's why I put that quote at the beginning of this chapter. It's from a song that used to play all the time on the radio in the '80s. The thing is, people don't always know what they want, even when they think they do. I can't tell you how many times I've worked with a client who is absolutely, 100 percent convinced they want one thing, and they end up with something completely different. The only way to figure out what they really want and, more importantly, to help *them* figure out what they really want is by not making it about

51

you and what you want to sell and instead asking the right questions at the right time.

Those questions help me look at a home or a situation and see not only *if* it can work but *how*, which sometimes means seeing things a little (or a lot) differently than the way they appear. I've always been able to do that, ever since I bought that first townhouse in Tanglewood and ever since I looked at my fork and imagined it as a pulley and drove my mother half crazy. The challenge is in helping other people see what I see, even if it's not exactly visible. When it works out, they end up falling in love with something they never would have considered, had I not asked one specific question or another.

But the other crucial component to this equation is honesty.

The other reason a lot of people are uncomfortable selling—and maybe this applies to you—is because they feel like, to do it right, they have to lie or at least stretch or misrepresent the truth in a way that kind of feels like lying. I think that's just wrong. *Big* mistake. Huge. It's so much easier to just say the truth. I always have, even at a young age.

So when I was hiring doctors for Guam and Saipan, I was honest. It was just easier. They would ask me the salary, and I would reply, "Oh, it's on the low side." They would ask what the cost of living was, and I would reply, "It's crazy high, and the houses aren't even very cute!" And then I would just say nothing.

And of course, at some point, the recruit would ask, "Then why would I want to go?"

And I would say, "I have no idea, but the doctors that I have sent seem to value recess as much as they do medicine." And that's when I'd explain how Micronesia was a springboard to many amazing places, which was nice because, as I mentioned, the housing was not very cute.

At the same time, I would ask them questions like "How often do you eat tomatoes?"

Usually they would look at me in confusion and say, "Tomatoes?"

"Yes, tomatoes," I'd reply. "If you were having friends over and planning to serve a salad and Guam happened to be out of tomatoes, would that send you over the edge?"

They would laugh, thinking I was joking, but I wasn't. Guam was, in fact, frequently out of tomatoes and other things people in the States are used to having around.

Then I'd say, "Now that I have your attention, how do you feel about snakes?"

It went on and on. It was fun to catch them off guard. But the point was I got to the truth, and so did they. The ads I ran in the *New England Journal of Medicine* were equally direct and honest. Once, after Guam was hit with a huge typhoon, my ad read "Okay, so you may have a few bad-hair days—but when you are not practicing medicine, the scuba diving is pretty awesome." I never lied about the downside of the job.

I wound up hiring more than thirty doctors to move to Micronesia before I ever saw the place myself; however, I did some intense studying (kind of like my mother did when she applied for that job at McDonnell Douglas) and was able to ask the right questions, to the point that people thought I had lived there. In other words, I did my homework. And real estate is no different. By the time I got my license, I had already studied many of the buildings on the Upper East Side and memorized the lay of the land, when they were built, the architects, and the average price per square foot. That knowledge helped me build confidence when I got started, and it paid off.

Dr. Gumbiner was so impressed that he started inviting me into board meetings and sit-downs with prominent doctors and executives in Southern California. Eventually, he had me regularly traveling to Guam, so I finally got to experience what I was talking about firsthand and explore the whole Micronesia chain.

It was a great chapter in my life. What began as a summer job had developed into an exciting career that I loved.

And the best part was learning that, out of over a hundred doctors I wound up recruiting to move to Guam or Saipan, the vast majority signed up for a second contract. That meant they were happy. They didn't want to quit or come home. I had matched them with a lifestyle that they loved, and that made me happy. In fact, I still keep in touch with many of the doctors to this day. I even had the pleasure of hosting one of them, Dr. Catherine Kurosu, to showcase her just-published book, *True Wellness: How to Combine the Best of Western and Eastern Medicine for Optimal Health*, at one of my listings on Central Park. How great is that? I was able to succeed for them, for Dr. Gumbiner, and also for myself, just by being honest about what their lifestyle would entail and identifying the right matches.

● ● ●

I don't see any difference in real estate. Recently, I was invited to work on a new development project late in the process. I was sitting in a room with architects, investors, and developers, when they excitedly revealed their latest vision and plan for a soon-to-be residential condo. And then I heard the dreaded question: "Vickey, what do you think?"

What did I think? In my head, I was saying, *I know what I think, but they are not going to want to hear it.* I don't like to hurt people's feelings, but when they ask for my opinion, they are going to get it. I knew I had to give an answer. So I turned and said, "Gentlemen, I am not sure how to sell that. Is there an option B?"

You can imagine the feeling in the room. But my belief is, *Better to speak the truth now if I can save someone from a train wreck later.* I might risk losing the project, but if I don't believe in the project, that's a risk I am willing to take.

I once showed an apartment to a woman who loved it so much she sent her husband to look at it the next day. I was confused. I thought the place was awful. But when we went outside, the husband looked at me all excited and said, "This is going to go fast, right? Should we offer above the ask?"

Above ask? Seriously, I was speechless.

He said, "Vickey? Why are you so quiet?"

I shook my head and told him I was sorry. I wasn't sure how to respond.

He said, "What are you thinking?"

"Well, I see how you must like the size." It was two apartments combined into one, so it was very large. He agreed that, yes, he did like the size, at which point I said, "It's kind of like a large, acrylic sweater."

"As opposed to?" he asked.

"A cashmere sweater. The fiber of this apartment is cheap."

He laughed and said, "How do you really feel?"

That's when I finally spoke up and gave him my full, honest assessment—that the renovation felt disjointed, the windows were small, and the view was of the equipment on top of the neighboring building. But, yes, it was big! We found them something else, and when we closed, he sent me a beautiful Herman Miller desk chair with a thank-you note: *You are honest, smart, and caring. Thank you for helping us through this complex process of finding our home.*

It's bringing people and places together.

Back when I first started in real estate, after I was named Rookie of the Year, the head of the firm asked me, "Vickey, what did you do before real estate?"

And I very proudly said, "Oh, I put together healthcare groups in Southern California and on the islands of Guam and Saipan."

"What the hell does that have to do with real estate in New York City?" he asked.

And I said, "Alan, everything. It's bringing people and places together."

It's asking questions and understanding people and being able to tell if something is the right fit for them. And it's always being direct and honest, even if it looks like that honesty might not get me what I want.

That's how I get to make dreams come true. And I promise, if I can do it, you can do it too.

CHAPTER 5

"Can I Sit Down with You for Twenty Minutes?"

"After the final no there comes a yes and on that yes the future of the world hangs."

—WALLACE STEVENS

Dr. Gumbiner's company, FHP, grew into a pretty big deal in the medical field, and the senior plan ended up being the largest HMO contract for Medicare. FHP went from a small start-up to a Fortune 500 company. It got so big that a large healthcare firm, called Pacificare, bought them for $2.1 billion, and all of a sudden, I was working for Pacificare. While they had some interesting ideas for my future, I had a better idea.

So I told Pacificare, "I will open up my own firm. I'll contract with you"—because they still needed me to hire doctors for Guam and Saipan—"and I'll sign contracts with the hospital on the island."

I ended up recruiting people to work for me and opened up my own firm. My partner Gary also opened up his own firm and specialized in recruiting medical directors.

Then, as life would have it, that's when my husband got relocated. He had a choice of going to Denver or New York City, and I said, "I vote New York." We sold our house and got our youngest daughter, Pacey, out of school (our oldest daughter, Teka, was already in college), and we moved to Manhattan.

Once I got there, reality set in pretty quick. I didn't know a single person in New York. I was on the phone between California and Guam, and the time difference was not easy. Work became a challenge. I went on for a while like this and thought, *I'm not getting out of the apartment, and I'm way too close to my refrigerator.* We were only going to be in New York for two years—that was the original plan—and so far, it was looking like I wasn't even going to get to experience it. So I decided: *It's time for a change. I want to pivot and do something different.*

That was the beginning of my real estate career.

• • •

Back in California, everyone used to tell me I should get my real estate license. But I loved my career as a physician recruiter, so I was content with fixing up a new house and selling it every few years. In New York, the possibilities were endless, and when I thought about it, real estate was the perfect career for me. If I got my real estate license, I'd have to get to know the city as part of my job. So I took the course and got my license and started looking for a place to work, and I was eventually offered a position at a firm that was then known as Halstead Properties.

The offer was extremely tempting. We were living on Eightieth and Madison, right by the Metropolitan Museum of Art, and the office for this firm was literally across the street. It was so close that when Pacey came home from school, I could run home and make her a tuna melt and run right back to the office. Who gets to do that? I also loved the women who interviewed me at Halstead: Elizabeth, the manager, and Diane, the owner of the firm. They were just lovely, and they offered me the position right out of the gate, which meant they could actually see how a successful physician recruiter might make an equally successful real estate broker.

But I figured I should at least interview at one other office. So, since Halstead was more of a boutique firm, I decided I should try a big, corporate firm. I was used to a corporate environment after working with Dr. Gumbiner and Pacificare. So I called the biggest agency in town—Douglas Elliman, in Midtown Manhattan—to ask for an interview.

The office manager on the phone asked what my background was. When I told her about my work recruiting doctors, she immediately replied, "Um ... we don't have a desk."

You can probably guess what *didn't* happen next.

I didn't hang up. Yes, that's what most people would do. But we've already established that I march to the beat of a different drum.

Instead, I said, "Wow! You must be doing really well—that you don't have a desk." And then I said, "So do you mind if I ask you a question?"

She said I could.

"Could I come in and sit down with you, face-to-face? I promise I won't take much of your time. And if it's a match, then I don't mind waiting for a desk to open up. And if it's not a match, then I'll accept the position that was already offered to me."

That's how I got in the door at Douglas Elliman. I was able to convince the office manager, whose name was Susan, to meet with me face-to-face just because I asked her to. Again, it didn't happen because I have magical powers. It happened because, just by asking honestly for what I wanted, I demonstrated that I was confident and not easily discouraged. Those are qualities that are important for any position, but especially a *sales* position.

So I got on the subway and went to Midtown and sat down in front of Susan. And, wouldn't you know it, the first question out of her mouth was "Do you have your résumé?"

I demonstrated that I was confident and not easily discouraged. Those are qualities that are important for any position, but especially a *sales* position.

I hadn't brought a résumé.

"You don't have a desk," I explained. "I didn't think it was an interview; I thought we were doing a friendly introduction. I'm an open book, so ask me anything." We started chatting. She asked me a few questions, but I ended up asking her a lot more questions than she asked me.

I approached her the same way I approached Dr. Gumbiner back when I was just a kid curious about a possible summer job. I was genuinely curious about what working at a big, corporate real estate office would be like and how it would be different than working with the lovely women at Halstead and if it might be a better fit for me. Although, at that moment, I was even more curious about the fact that Susan told me they didn't have a desk—because, as I looked around the office, I couldn't help noticing most of those supposedly full desks were empty.

So I said, "I know you said you don't have a desk available. I'm just curious, if you don't mind me asking, where are all the agents right now? Are they selling apartments? Are they sleeping in, or are they shopping? Where are they?"

Susan laughed because, as I know now, she had no idea where those agents were, and she was pretty sure they weren't all out there selling apartments.

Once that was out of the way, I moved into my other questions. Since I was new to the world of real estate, I wanted to know how the business worked. So I asked Susan to describe the company's top five agents and what their skill sets were. It was a lot like when I asked the man in the suit about the salespeople selling the FHP health plans. I wanted to know what it took to do well at the job and, of course, if I would have fun doing it.

Susan looked surprised to be asked that question. Most people would have used that time to tell her about all of their accomplishments, not because they're self-centered but because they think, in order to get a job, they have to use the time they were lucky enough to secure to sell themselves. I'm sure Susan expected me to talk about what a great physician recruiter I was and how I helped build Dr. Gumbiner's business into a powerhouse in the healthcare field. By not talking about myself but asking questions about the position, I demonstrated that I really cared about the job, about how to do it well, and, ultimately, about how I might make Susan's life easier.

She described a few of their best-performing agents and explained why they were successful. And when she was done, I said, "Now talk to me about the five agents that are about to lose their desk. What do they have in common, and why are they not producing?"

I wasn't trying to get Susan to insult any of her salespeople. But I was definitely curious about what type of person does not make a good real estate agent and what those people might do wrong. Of course, asking Susan about her worst performers also got her thinking about the people she would like to replace and what it might be like to have a person like me working there instead.

"Now, I'm also curious," I said. "What percent of your agents did something else professionally before real estate?" By the way, I think 95 percent of agents come from another field, but I didn't know that at the time, so the question came from an honest place. It also reminded her that everyone starts out somewhere (and, yes, that includes you).

Then I asked her five more questions.

She finally just started laughing and said, "You are hilarious."

"No, I'm just curious."

I really wasn't trying to be obnoxious. I was trying to wrap my head around the industry and how it all worked. After all, opportunities to pick the brain of the manager of the biggest real estate office in New York City don't usually fall into your lap. But it would be dishonest if I said that I didn't also use the opportunity to showcase myself in the best possible way—by showing that I was interested and eager to learn. This probably explains why Susan finally looked at me and said, "You know what, Vickey? I like you a lot, and you are going to be fantastic. I know I said I didn't have a desk. I will find a desk for you. Please join us."

This led to another dilemma. I had already been offered a job by the women at Halstead. And it was right across from my apartment! So while I was thrilled, I said, "Oh my gosh! I can't tell you what that means to me and how grateful I am. But, the truth of the matter is, I really need to digest all this valuable information you've just given me, and I will need a couple of days, and then I'll make my decision and get back to you. Is that okay?"

Susan started laughing and said, "I knew you were going to say that. Who offered you a job?" I told her it was Halstead, and it turned out she had worked for Halstead. She told me a little about them, and then she said, "You need to be here. You need to be here." Yes, she actually said it twice. She was clearly convinced.

I said, "I appreciate that, but I still need to think about it, and I promise I'll let you know on Monday."

The next day, Susan called and said, "I don't want to wait until Monday. Please accept our offer. I will help you. You're going to be fantastic. Come to us."

I said, "I do, again, appreciate that, but I still want to give a final answer on Monday."

I was not toying with her. Real estate was a new career for me. New York was a new city for me. I really needed to weigh all the pros and cons and consult my gut. After I did all that, I decided I was going to go with Douglas Elliman. I knew it was the right decision, but it also meant I had to tell Elizabeth and Diane that I was taking another job, and that wasn't going to be any fun knowing they really wanted me at their firm.

But I had to go with my gut: "I feel so bad because I appreciate the opportunity, but, in my heart of hearts, I'm kind of feeling like I need the big name behind me because no one knows me in New York."

• • •

When I first started at my new firm, I had to go through training. Right away, they sent us home with an assignment to call three "For Sale by Owners"—which, if you're reading this and don't happen to be in real estate, means I had to contact three people who were selling their property on their own, without a real estate agent. I went home that night, and I procrastinated. I was helping Pacey with her homework and getting dinner ready. Then I looked at the clock. It was nine o'clock at night, and I realized, *Holy cow—I forgot to do my homework.*

My very first assignment, and I completely forgot. But I couldn't lie—I wasn't going to walk into class and say I did something if I didn't. I couldn't just not do it, because that would be disrespectful, and it's not my way to not do the work I'm asked to do. The only possible solution I could think to do was to grab the phone, grab the paper, go to the "For Sale by Owner" section, and make three phone calls.

I made my first call. I got voice mail. The message said, "Hi. You've reached John and Mary. We're not home right now. If you're calling about the apartment, please leave your name and number. No brokers, please. (Beep.)"

No brokers, please. That's what the machine said.

But I was just doing my homework, not offering my services. So I said, "Hi, John. Hi, Mary. It's me, Vickey. I have a dilemma right now because I did hear you say 'no brokers,' and I am, well, a broker. But don't hang up please because I simply have a question for you, and I promise it will be painless—if you would be kind enough to write my number down and call me tomorrow, preferably before 1:00 p.m. that would be great." I left my phone number, hung up, and thought, *One down, two to go.*

The next day in class, the person who was teaching called on me and asked what my experience was. I told them about the voice mail, and the whole room started laughing. "Vickey, you poor thing," they said. "You're from California; this is New York. No one's going to call you back. You left your name after they said 'no brokers'?"

I sunk down in my seat and felt a little sad because I thought, *Why wouldn't they call me back? I was really polite and nice, and I think they'll call me back.*

Sure enough, at lunch break, I went back to my office, and the little red message button was lit up on the phone, and it was Mary. So I called her back.

Mary wasn't exactly polite. She said, "Hi, this is Mary. Yeah. You called, and you said you had a question. What is it?"

Well, I didn't know. I hadn't planned that far in advance. But I was just so excited that she called me back. I said, "Mary, you have no idea how happy I am to talk to you." She still wasn't very polite, but I said, "I just have a couple of questions for you." And I literally had to think on my feet what those questions could possibly be. I had been in real estate for all of two days and didn't even have a business card! But I had paid attention in real estate class and had already done my own apartment search in New York City, so I had some understanding of what mattered to buyers.

So I said, "You know, I noticed in the paper you were holding an open house on Sunday, and I was trying to wrap my head around the L line. You're in 15L, yes?"

She said she was.

"I can't recall which way that faces. Is that south facing? East facing?"

"Oh, the L line? We're south facing, and we get sun all day long. It's the best line in the whole building."

"Amazing," I said. "Everyone loves sunshine. That's fantastic. You're facing south."

"Well, is that all you wanted to know?"

And I said, "No, no, no, no. The real question is, do you mind just talking to me about your kitchen?"

"My kitchen?"

"Yeah. Buyers always want to know about kitchens. I don't know why—because most of them don't even cook."

And suddenly, Mary warmed up to me and started going on and on about her amazing kitchen. "Oh, we renovated our kitchen. We have a window in there, granite countertops, stainless steel Miele appliances …"

I needed to buy time and figure out my next move, so I repeated what she said. "Granite countertops. Amazing! What'd you do on your backsplash?"

"Oh, I have these beautiful tiles on the backsplash …"

"And a window in the kitchen? That's unusual."

"Tell me about it."

"And stainless steel appliances. That sounds amazing! So, did you sell your apartment on Sunday?"

She said no.

"Wait a minute," I said. "Southern exposure, windowed kitchen, granite countertops. What's wrong with these people?"

She started laughing and said, "I don't know. We had about thirty people through, but no one bought it." Then she said, "I suppose you have a buyer."

And she kind of went back to being not so nice when she said that.

I was thinking, *Lady, I don't even have a business card.* But I didn't say that. I said, "You know what, Mary? With that kitchen and the southern exposure, I really, really wish I could tell you I do have a buyer, but the truth is I don't have a buyer today, but it doesn't mean I won't have one tomorrow. Can I ask you one last question? And promise not to hit me on the head."

She said sure.

I said, "Is there any way I could just peek in and see the apartment? Because if I see it and then come across someone, at least I can tell them I've seen it with my own eyes. Because what you've described is amazing."

She said, "Absolutely. Come by at 4:30."

When I showed up, I did the opposite of what every other agent does. I didn't bring a whole pile of sales materials to hopefully convince John and Mary to list their apartment with me. (I couldn't! Remember: I still didn't have a business card.) However, I did bring a notepad. I showed up and introduced myself. And just like I used to do selling health plans in LA, I paid attention to the details.

There happened to be a vase that was absolutely exquisite. I said, "That's an amazing vase. Where did you get it?" Well, it turned out Mary really loved this vase. She told me how it had been done by an artist, how she got it when she was in New Mexico, and on and on. I said, "It's a really stunning vase. Before we sit down, do you mind if I walk through the apartment with you?"

Mary didn't object and started leading me through the apartment. I pulled out my notepad and started taking notes. How many closets? How big were the bedrooms? I tried to get as complete a picture of the apartment as I could.

Then I said, "Mary, you know what? Can I ask you another question?"

She said, "Yeah."

"How did you come up with your price?"

"Well, you know, we went through what has sold"—meaning they came up with their price by looking at comparable sales in their area (a method I don't always think is the best for pricing, but we'll get to that later).

So I said, "Oftentimes, we hear about new listings first. If a property is coming up in your building or close by, it could have value to you. Would it help you if I at least shared that information?"

"Oh absolutely! That'd be so kind of you."

"Also, do you mind if I give you just a couple of tips? Because you are having another open house Sunday, right?"

She said I could.

I said, "Everything looks perfect, but sometimes a fresh eye can bring something new to the table. I'd open those blinds all the way up—let even more sunshine in. And we all have the stack of stuff that I'm seeing to the left of your sofa. I would tuck that away during the open house. Just try to make as clean a palette as possible. But it shows so well. You've done a great job!" I gave her a thumbs-up and said, "You're going to sell it this Sunday for sure. And I'll keep you posted if I hear anything about some other listings."

> **Everything looks perfect but sometimes a fresh eye can bring something new to the table.**

She thanked me and asked for my card. I told her I forgot to bring one and wrote my name down on a piece of paper from my notepad.

She called me two weeks later. She and her husband had decided to look for an agent after all. They were interviewing five people, and I made the cut.

This time when I showed up at their apartment, I brought a packet of sales material—because they had made the choice to invite me to interview, meaning they wanted to know how I would sell their house. (I also had a card.) I ended up getting the listing—because I was patient, because I asked questions that showed Mary that I was interested in her and her property, and, of course, because I didn't let the word "no" stop me. Just like the situation with the tile guy when I was redoing my first condo, the fact that a person says no one minute doesn't mean they'll still feel that way later. That's why I always make sure to leave the door open to new possibilities.

• • •

That former For Sale by Owner (the first of many), who I called during my first training assignment, was actually not my first listing. During those two weeks between when I first visited the apartment and when Mary invited me back, I was on the phone trying to raise money for my daughter's school, and I really clicked with this one woman.

She said, "You are so nice. We should get together for coffee. Do you work?"

I told her I just got my real estate license, which gave me some flexibility with my schedule, and that I would love to meet her.

"Oh, real estate," she said. "We have two sons and just adopted a little girl, and we're in a two-bedroom now. We really need to move into a three- or four-bedroom, but the thought of that process just gives me a headache."

I said, "I have a great idea. Since I have so much time on my hands and I love looking at real estate, why don't I pull up some three- and four-bedroom listings. We'll meet for coffee and go look at some of them, and it'll give you an understanding of what it costs to move into an apartment that size. Does that make sense to you?"

She said that it did, so we made an appointment and had coffee and went out and looked at apartments. Then we went back to her apartment so I could check out what she would be selling. The place was renovated, but it didn't look very cute. She only had one section of a sectional, no end tables, no rug, not one piece of art on the wall—and *a lot* of toys on the floor.

"When you sell this," I said, "we need to dress it up."

"You know what, Vickey? It's not my forte. The thought of going to buy a pillow is enough to throw me overboard. It's not my skill set."

So I said, "I'll do it for you."

She was surprised by that. "What do you mean you'll do it?"

"We'll just go out together. I'll get you a whole sofa. I'll get some end tables—you're going to need them wherever you move anyway, and you're definitely going to need them to sell this apartment." She didn't know about my June Cleaver fantasies and how much I love fixing places up.

I took her out. We went shopping, and then, each day, new stuff would get delivered to her apartment. Her husband, naturally, noticed that his apartment was slowly transforming into a home worthy of some modern-day Cleavers and wanted to know what was happening as the place never looked so good. She had told him that she met me, a new friend and real estate agent, and I was helping her fix up their house.

Well, he wanted to meet me. So we set up a time, and the first thing he said was, "Listen. My wife couldn't be happier. Happy wife, happy life. She thinks you walk on water. But ..." And he suddenly leaned into my face—very aggressively. "I own my own company," he said. "How long have you been in the business? Eight days now? Why would I possibly give you an over $2 million listing?"

But I didn't let his aggression scare me or stop me.

Instead, I held up three fingers in front of his face (which, as I mentioned, was suddenly much closer to me than was really comfortable) and said, with the straightest face, "For three very good reasons."

He smirked.

"Number one," I said, "I'm under a great umbrella with my firm—they offer me the protection and all the tools necessary to help navigate us all through this process. Number two, I am willing to bring on the number-two agent in my office for you as insurance. But the truth is, number three, I'll be holding that umbrella, and I simply bring magic."

Suddenly, Mr. Aggressive was a little less aggressive. "You didn't even blink," he said.

I looked him straight in the eye and said, "Nor did you."

Then he laughed and hired me. And that's how I got my first listing.

I think it comes down to two things, neither of which are magic:

1. I demonstrated my work ethic and got to know my client and her needs before I so much as suggested she hire me to work for her. I let her get to know me and come to the decision on her own. (Note: Don't talk about your value; show your value.)

2. I showed her husband that I was confident, professional, and not afraid. Since I was new to the field, I knew I had to win his respect in order to get the listing, so I made sure that I kept my cool.

So my real estate career was off and running. I had my first listing, and it was time to get ready for my first open house. I had let my inner June Cleaver go crazy and helped my new friend transform her apartment into a showplace. The artwork was on the walls. I had the candles lit. It looked beautiful. All systems go.

The doorman buzzed up and said, "Your buyers are here."

My client's baby had the stomach flu, with explosive diarrhea, so she was in the bedroom changing her. It was winter, and a blizzard had come in out of nowhere, so her son ran out on the terrace to play in the snow, running in circles with his arms out wide and his head up, catching the snow in his mouth, as kids do.

My client started yelling, "Come inside! Come inside!" But she had to deal with the baby, so she said, "Vickey, can you get him inside?"

So I said, "You have to come in, honey," and he finally ran inside.

Well, the first thing he must have seen were the candles burning. And I guess he got frightened and ran over and blew out the candles on the dining table, and the hot wax went everywhere, and that scared him even more.

I was saying, "No, no," as calmly as I could, but he ran down the hallway and accidentally knocked a brand-new piece of artwork off the wall, causing glass to shatter all over the floor.

They also had a cat. I had brought flowers, which the cat proceeded to eat and then promptly vomited on the floor.

And then the doorbell rang.

I had a baby with diarrhea in one room, an upset kid, snow all over, melted wax on the table, and a pile of flowery vomit. It was my first open house ever. Seriously, you can't make this up.

I opened the door and said, "I'm so sorry. Can you just give me like five minutes? I'll explain in a moment." I shut the door as politely as I could and just left the buyers standing there. I got the broom and swept up the glass. I picked up the vomit, threw it in the garbage. The wax was still on the table, but we couldn't deal with that. My client grabbed her children, ran out the side door, and I opened the front door and said, "Welcome!"—like nothing had happened. I wound up selling the apartment at full price within a week.

If you haven't been working in real estate for a while, that might sound crazy or impossible or like the kind of thing that *never* happens to you. I swear it can. Again, it's not that I have magic powers; it's that I work hard and figure out how to make it happen. And, I promise, you can do it too.

CHAPTER 6

"Did You Practice Your Presentation?"

"You have to believe in yourself when no one else does—
that makes you a winner right there."

—VENUS WILLIAMS

Not long after I made that first sale, a more experienced broker from my office invited me to go out with her on a listing pitch. We were riding up in the elevator to the apartment, and she was visibly nervous. She asked me if I too was nervous.

But I wasn't. I don't get nervous very often. I trust things will work out in the end as long as I let them. So I was being honest when I asked my colleague, "Why would I be nervous?"

She asked, "Did you practice your presentation?"

Oh. *That* was why I would be nervous.

I admitted that I had not practiced the presentation, and this made her even more nervous.

"What will you say when we get into the woman's living room?" she asked.

This confused me. "How can I know what I'm going to say if I don't even know who she is yet?"

To be honest, I hadn't really considered using a memorized script or memorized *anything*. Ever since I had to go door to door reading a preset spiel about FHP health plans and wound up getting expletives and shoes thrown at me, I've had pretty strong feelings about not approaching people with scripts and lists of facts and figures. During those two-plus decades I spent in healthcare, I had always relied on my ability to understand a person quickly and ask the right questions to help me connect with them and understand their needs. I made our interactions about them and not about me, which meant not memorizing a script about what I was offering them. And it usually seemed to work. It worked with welfare recipients. It worked with doctors. Why wouldn't it work in real estate?

My more experienced associate thought I was a little crazy. She had a million reasons why we needed to follow the script, and they all made sense. We were talking about multimillion-dollar properties, not healthcare plans. What could be more important than a well-constructed presentation that demonstrated you had all the facts and figures, which proved you could sell that property for top dollar, right at your fingertips? The poor woman had spent hours perfecting and rehearsing her presentation, and I was just planning to … what? To *wing it*? No wonder she was nervous.

Except I wasn't exactly winging it. I may not memorize a whole presentation, but I do spend a lot of time studying and going to open houses and looking up facts. I get a full understanding of the lay of the land. For example, I always tell brokers, "You can't price an apartment by just saying 'It's sixteen hundred square feet.' You have to peel that onion back and really know that building." You have to understand the infrastructure, the systems, the financials, whether or not there's a reserve fund—there are a million questions, to study and really know and understand, to decide what a property is "worth."

I just didn't (and still don't) think *reciting* all those facts and figures is an especially effective way to form a connection with a potential client and demonstrate what working with you might be like.

However, at this point, I was still new to the game, and because of that, my more experienced associate's nervousness was starting to make me nervous. I had always done well doing things my way, but I had to wonder: *Had I missed something crucial? Was I going about this real estate thing all wrong?*

We got to the prospective client's apartment, and she opened the door to greet us. That's when I saw it, proudly mounted on a wall: a wooden storyboard of—no joke!—Guam, Saipan, and the other islands of Micronesia. Seriously! What were the chances?

Of course, I said hello and quickly and enthusiastically asked the woman about the storyboard, and we immediately started sharing stories about Guam and Saipan.

To me, the real "presentation" is always about presenting yourself and how you can help somebody.

Once we were inside, I noticed a book on the woman's bookshelf, and that led into another conversation about a whole other topic. We didn't talk much about pricing or numbers, but we weren't just chatting either. The whole time, I was asking questions to help me understand this potential client's needs.

By the time our meeting was over, we had spent almost no time on the presentation my associate worked so hard on. Instead, we talked about what our potential client cared about and needed and about how we might help make that happen.

When we left the apartment, my associate told me she was impressed by "what I just did" in the meeting. But, again, "what I just did" wasn't magic. I just did the same thing I've been doing since I sold my first FHP health plan when I was eighteen years old. To me, the real "presentation" is always about presenting yourself and how you can help somebody, and the first step in doing that is connecting. It's about showing a person that you really *see* them, that you're interested in and attuned to what matters to them, not attached to some preconceived idea of what they need that you came up with in a script.

After all, every single person is different. Every person has different needs. And the best way to find out what those needs are is to ask the right questions—which may have you asking, "Okay, Vickey. So how am I supposed to figure out what the right questions are?" For me, it's always come down to using my powers of observation—although I would have had to be blindfolded to miss that storyboard of Guam and Saipan! People tell us who they are. The problem is we choose not to listen.

• • •

As I mentioned earlier, one thing I've always been great at is noticing details, which may not be a skill they teach in school, but it's still one that has served me very well in the real world and goes back as far as I can remember.

Back when I was twelve years old, my mom said, while reminiscing about our childhood in the beach cities of Southern California, "Vickey, remember when we lived in Hermosa Beach? Remember that little girl you used to play with in the duplex in the back?"

I must have been six at the time, but I remembered vividly. "Oh, yeah," I said. "The girl whose pinky toe kind of curled up a little." My mother and sister both looked at me like I had lost my mind.

I thought, *How could you not remember that? She used to walk around barefoot, and that little pinky toe was sticking up.*

It was difficult for me to understand, especially as a child, that people didn't see the exact same thing I saw when I looked at something. I didn't see my eye for detail as some kind of superpower; I saw it as, I don't know, seeing! I genuinely assumed it worked the same way for everyone. But it doesn't. And once I figured that out, my powers of observation began to set me apart in a good way, as opposed to just a weirdo way. They're my window into finding that little something that allows me to connect with somebody. (Note: Always walk through life with your eyes open.)

And again, even if my powers of observation are some kind of superpower, it's not like that superpower is exclusive to me. When you're not thinking about yourself and worrying—about scripts or presentations, or how your hair looks, or if that last thing you said sounds stupid—and instead focus entirely on the other person, you can't help but notice details.

• • •

When I started out in real estate, the area where my eye for detail really set me apart and helped me serve my clients best was in helping people get their properties ready to sell. Remodeling so many houses of my own back in California taught me to look at any home or apartment and see what little tweaks could really make it shine. I could see what a place needed, what it didn't, and what changes would have the most impact. That skill alone helped me land my first listing, when I assisted that client, who only had one section of a sectional, turn her apartment into a showplace.

I knew this was a skill that set me apart. Keep in mind this was long before staging is what it is today. Every time I'd go to a new listing, I would look at it and take in the details: what should stay, what needed to be removed, what should be layered in to complement the property and make it show at its best. Then I would move furniture around and redo bookshelves, bring in different shower curtains and the right kind of soap, or, in the case of my friend from the phone, sometimes completely furnish the place—whatever a property needed to make it shine.

After a while, I started to develop a reputation in the business for knowing how to stage an apartment to sell for the highest price possible. Actually, it wasn't long at all. Within six months of beginning my real estate career, I got a call from CBS news asking if I'd be willing to do a segment on how to prepare your home for sale. Of course I agreed, and I shot a segment demonstrating some of my most important and impactful tips. It was so funny because the day my segment was on, they delayed it until the very end of the program so they could keep teasing it the whole way through. Every time they went to a commercial, one of the anchors would say, "Coming up: learn how to prepare your apartment to receive top dollar when you're selling, by Vickey Barron." So everyone who watched the news that night heard my name at least five times.

• • •

More recently, I had a listing for a penthouse that was not selling. (Yes, it happens to me too!) The owners really needed it sold, so they asked if it was time to lower the price. I knew they didn't need to do that, because I knew the price wasn't the problem. I knew I had to tell them something they probably didn't want to hear: "It's not the price; it's the furniture."

Now, to be honest, their furniture was perfectly lovely. They had every right to enjoy it and be proud of it, which I suppose is the reason I let it stay when I prepped the apartment in the first place. But when it came to what buyers in this particular area expected to see, it just wasn't the right vibe. This was a beautifully renovated home in a funky, artistic part of New York City. My clients' furniture was telling a completely different story. Buyers couldn't picture themselves living in the home. It didn't appeal to their emotions.

These clients were not interested in buying all new furniture, but I was so confident that, once it told the right story, their home was going to sell. So much so that I offered to do it for them, from soup to nuts. They were shocked, but I promised to keep the receipts so they could reimburse me after the place sold. I knew it would.

They removed all their belongings, and I went to work. I brought in everything: furniture, rugs, art. I even created an art room, with an antique art cart and supplies—to tell the perfect story of the cool, funky home buyers dream about. The transformation worked. I had three showings within the first week and sold the home for the asking price. It was kind of funny because, walking through the place, the buyer kept saying "I like these people" and "We could hang out. They have cool stuff." I couldn't lie to him. I had to tell him the place was staged, but that wound up giving the story an even happier ending. Since the furniture didn't belong to the owners, he was thrilled when he found out that he could buy 98 percent of it. It felt so good to be able to help my clients and get the place sold without losing money on a reduction in price. And I couldn't have done it if I was not willing to see the end before the beginning.

• • •

Another example of this was when six of us agents had volunteered to create a curriculum with the goal of raising the bar in the industry. The agents selected would go through a rigorous series of courses and receive a designation called NYRS. We were about to launch the course and were in desperate need of the right leader to teach the marketing section. We were all trying to identify the right individual when the light bulb came on, and I thought to myself that the perfect person would be Barbara Corcoran.

Well, when I presented my brilliant idea to the team of agents, they looked at me as if I were crazy.

One agent said, "Barbara Corcoran is never going to teach this class. She's onto bigger and better things. This is a ridiculous idea."

In my mind, it made all the sense in the world, and I saw her teaching it.

One of the agents said to me, "How well do you know her?"

I replied, "I've never met her before in my life, but I know of her, and I've read her book. I know she's great at marketing and believe she would enjoy teaching this class."

The team looked at me, and then another agent wagered that I couldn't get Barbara to teach the class. That was it; the bet was on.

I left that meeting, and about one week later, I was walking home from dinner on Park Avenue. It was drizzling and dark, but my eye caught a rickshaw with a woman getting out, not just any woman— but Barbara Corcoran!

I started yelling, "Barbara! Barbara! Stop!"

She stopped and looked at me, puzzled.

As I got closer to her, I said, "Hi, Barbara. It's me, Vickey Barron. I am an agent, and, unfortunately, I don't work at Corcoran,"—her old firm—"but I am involved at the Real Estate Board of New York. We're putting this course together and are in need of someone to lead the marketing portion of the class. I think you would be perfect to teach this class, and, the truth is, everyone on my team laughed at me when I suggested your name. They bet that I couldn't get you to teach this class, and I really, really hate to lose. So my question for you is, Would you help me and teach this first class for us?"

Barbara looked at me and said, "Let me see if I can get this straight. You have a bet that you can get me to teach the class. And if I agree to it, you win? And if I don't, you lose?"

"Yes. But I really, really hate to lose, so I really need you to teach this class." Barbara then asked me if there was any money involved, and I said, "No, unfortunately we don't have a budget to pay you to teach the class."

She said, "That's not what I meant. I meant, Is there a wager if you win or lose?"

"No. It was just a bit of fun. There's no money involved."

"Okay. Well, I asked because if there was money, I would want half of it!" she said and smiled. She's on *Shark Tank* for a reason! Then Barbara handed me her business card and said, "Why don't you email me tomorrow, and I'll give it some thought."

I emailed her the next day, and she agreed to teach the class.

What are the chances that I would stumble upon *the* Barbara Corcoran on Park Avenue at ten o'clock at night? And then what are the chances she would agree, as busy and successful as she is, to come to our little classroom and teach this class? But I feel that if you believe in something and see it happening and it makes sense, it is 100 percent possible. Again, this is making something happen instead of waiting for something to happen.

I realize this isn't easy for everyone. Getting people to believe in you takes self-confidence, and it can be hard to feel confident when things aren't going well. If that sounds like you, I have some advice, if you'll take it: lighten up on yourself.

If you've read this far (and if so, thank you for reading!), you've probably figured out that I don't worry very much about what other people think of me. I worry about being kind to them. I worry about treating them with respect and making sure I consider where they're coming from, even when they're not in the greatest mood or acting particularly kind themselves. But I don't worry about what they think of me.

I realize this is a gift. Maybe I was lucky that when I was growing up, my bar was low, so I had nowhere to go but up. So many people agonize over how other people perceive them—from how they look, to what they say, to the core of who they are. They miss opportunities that are right in front of them. They worry about looking silly, so they stay in the shadows, letting other people shine. I don't worry about making a complete fool of myself—and I've done it more than a few times. And now that I have several decades of life experience under my belt, I can honestly say the ability to laugh at myself and not take myself seriously is a big part of why I've come this far.

If you can learn to do that, too, you're halfway there.

CHAPTER 7

"Is He Having a Breakdown?"

"Nothing is good or bad, but thinking makes it so."

—WILLIAM SHAKESPEARE

My friend Gayle recently said something that really stuck with me. She said, "Vickey, the difference between you and me is you don't have fear." And she's right. You know that little voice most people have that tells them *Don't do it* when they approach something risky? Mine must have laryngitis or something. It's kind of hard to be afraid when you believe that, in the end, everything will turn out the way it is supposed to be and you will be okay.

The whole idea of me being fearless is kind of ironic, because my mother always saw me as this fragile, scared little girl who saw life through rose-colored glasses. What she didn't get (until that conversation at her deathbed) was that those rose-colored glasses were one of my strengths. I do tend to see the best in situations and in people, which could be why I don't have a temper. I have never been in a fight, or hit a person, or thrown anything at anyone.

But at the same time, someone once said to me, "You know what, Vickey? You very much believe there's right and wrong, and you're in it to *protect*." Well, you can't be a very good protector if you're afraid. Fear just gets in the way of doing what you have to do.

• • •

When I was fourteen, I was spending the night at a friend's house when a burglar broke in. Now, my friend, understandably, was terrified, and she went to hide in the closet. I immediately went into action mode, so I went to the stairwell and yelled at the top of my lungs, "Steve, get the gun!"

Well, there was no Steve and no gun, but the burglar didn't know that. He ran for his life straight out of that house.

I believe that, in life, you hit forks in the road, where there are two ways to go. If you go in the direction your fears tell you to go, you allow yourself to settle for less, to be bullied or taken advantage of, or to think the whole world's coming to an end. Or you can go the other way and say, "The world is a beautiful place. Everyone is amazing. We're in it together. We're going to make it to the end, and it's all going to be good." Obviously, in the story I just told, the world wasn't a beautiful place, and everyone wasn't amazing. When you need to figure out what to do next in a sticky situation, whether it's about holding on to a listing or getting rid of a would-be burglar, fear won't do you any good one way or another. The key is to keep your focus. Focus on the end result and what it will take to get there.

Believe me when I tell you: it can save your life.

• • •

Before moving to New York permanently, I was visiting with my daughter so she could interview for schools. As luck would have it, three days into the trip, she came down with the chickenpox and needed to quarantine for a week. Since we already checked out of the hotel but had the keys to our new, empty apartment, I decided I'd just go buy a blow-up mattress, pillows, and sheets, and we'd camp out and have a grand old time. I thought maybe it would be a good idea to get a TV, too, to keep her occupied.

After I purchased the TV, it dawned on me: *How do I get this back home?* A young man, seeing I was new to New York, told me to wave down a cab and successfully helped me get the TV into the trunk.

Then, shortly into my ride, the driver started screaming, "I'm gonna kill myself! I'm gonna kill myself!"—pounding the windshield and pulling at his steering wheel.

I thought to myself, *This man is either having a nervous breakdown, or he's trying to instill fear in me in hopes that I'll hop out the back seat and he'll take off with my brand-new TV.*

This was my "now what" moment.

Seeing an opening in the glass partition between the front and back seat, I reached in and patted the driver on the shoulder and asked, "What's your name?"

He said, "Tony."

"Tony, take a deep breath. We all have days like this. Talk to me about what's going on."

He shouted, "I can't take it anymore! I can't take it anymore!" and continued to beat his fists against the wheel.

"Tony, it's okay," I went on. "Just talk to me. I can see how complicated it is living in New York. We all have days like this. Now, what's happening? Do you have any children? How long have you been driving a cab?"

He seemed to be getting a little calmer. But then, just when I thought it was over, I saw him starting to escalate again.

At that point, I thought maybe I should write his license and name down in case something happened. So I looked down at the acrylic pocket for his name and license number. No license. My heart started pounding, and he must have seen that I was startled, because he reached back and felt that there was, in fact, no license.

This did not help things.

"This can't happen. Where is my license?" he screamed.

Right in the middle of the road, he put the car in park, opened the door, got out, and started searching around the front seat to look for his license. The guy's pants were falling down, butt crack exposed, cars all honking around him in the middle of 5:30 p.m. weekday bumper-to-bumper traffic in the middle of Manhattan. It was quite the scene.

I said, "Get in the car. Don't worry. Get in the car, and we'll figure this out."

He proceeded to get back into the car, and we made our way up Madison Avenue. I honestly could not believe it was happening. *Is this the real cabdriver? Or did he mug the real cabdriver, and he's trying to take me and the TV with him?* I didn't know.

All I know is I kept him talking about his problems. "I have to go to court next week because a passenger filed a complaint about me taking a long path to Brooklyn to deliberately rack up the bill. This is not my first offense, and my mother-in-law is going to be sitting in the courtroom. When I see her, I'm going to punch her in the face."

Interesting, I thought to myself. *Talking about getting violent with a woman.*

I needed to get his attention, so I said, "Look me in the eyes."

He looked at me.

"I've so been where you are. Trust me, Tony. I've been there. It's all going to be okay. Just take a deep breath, and keep your eyes on the road. It's all going to be okay."

We finally pulled up to Eightieth and Madison. The doorman approached and unloaded the TV. I left a hefty tip, and Tony was on his way. He was probably puzzled, thinking that he picked up a whack job. Most people would have fed into the fear, but I was curious and concerned that he was acting that way. It was not healthy.

Honestly, to this day, I don't know what his motive was. Was he in need of a TV, or was he having a serious mental breakdown? All I know for sure is that, in that situation and in so many others, it is all about compassion.

Later, my colleague Jose said, "You know the difference between you and me? I'd hand the guy twenty bucks and run out the door, but you sit in the back seat and try to analyze the guy and protect your TV."

You can choose to see the glass as half empty or half full, or you can just *know* there's a pitcher around the corner that's going to fill your glass to the brim.

Now, I get that this is a pretty extreme experience (although there have been others, some of which you'll read about very soon) and maybe not the best example to use to talk about the kind of fear people deal with on a daily basis. But I dealt with that fear the way I basically deal with all fears: by taking the time to really think and process, visualize, and then take action. If I had succumbed to analysis paralysis—where you worry about the decision you have to make so long you don't make it—who knows what would have happened to us?

The other thing I did in that situation—something I use a lot in other less threatening situations—was change the energy. Well, that same ability to pivot on a dime has helped me a lot in my career (and my life). It's not that I don't have failures or make mistakes. It's not that I've never lost a $50 million listing or disappointed an important client. Of course I have. Everyone at this level in my business has. But I look at those moments as just a normal, day-to-day aspect of my job and, really, of life. So I don't dwell on them. Because, seriously, what's the point of dwelling on what went wrong or what didn't work out when there are so many opportunities for things to go right and work out? That's where I focus my energy. I don't even think about it. It's automatic.

I know it's not like that for everyone. I had a head start, growing up in a household where the energy was bad a lot of the time because people were stressed out and unhappy. I guess that's where I learned the power of doing something completely off the wall, like creating a real estate rap song and singing it in an interview. I did that kind of thing at home all the time. People would be angry or upset, and I'd make somebody laugh and break the tension. It would help. I still do it in my daily life, too, and in real estate.

I think, in the end, what it all comes down to is the power of the mind. You get to choose the way you see things. You can choose to be afraid or not to be afraid. You can choose to see the glass as half empty or half full, or you can just *know* there's a pitcher around the corner that's going to fill your glass to the brim. That last one has always been my approach to life.

• • •

I can remember dancing in my room at age ten with my beautiful new shoes (which had actually been handed down to me by a girl down the street), envisioning the amazing life I was going to have. Did my mom or my sister or any of my relatives see that life for me? Of course not. But that visualization, that thought process, and dreaming big gave me energy and hope. *Life is going to be great! Period. End of story!*

Because ... why wouldn't it be?

Honestly, I think if everybody worked on their thought process the way they work on their bodies or their careers, the world would be a better place. The mind is a terrible thing to waste, but so many of us do, letting fear hold us back from what we want (or need) to do, dwelling on the negative when there are so many possibilities out there. And sometimes, making the tiniest little tweak to our thinking can work wonders.

For example (and this is a work-related example), I had an apartment listed that was just not selling, no matter what I did. I had done everything: staging, broker events, marketing, open houses— the full gamut of services. I felt confident. When I looked at the apartment and gave it my complete, honest assessment, I really saw it selling. I knew it would sell. Why wouldn't it sell?

It didn't sell.

Seriously, I could not catch a break. Every other apartment on the market that had similar comps seemed like it was getting sold except mine. What could possibly be going wrong? I racked my brain, but I just couldn't figure it out.

Then I had an aha moment. I thought back through the conversations I had with the owners of the apartment, replaying them in my mind. And what did I hear? A lot of worrying about how the apartment was overpriced and on a low floor and how it was never going to sell because all the other apartments were so much better. Seriously, these people thought they were cursed. And the thing is, they were right—not because of their apartment but because of their *mindset*.

Once I figured that out, I called a meeting. Maybe it was more like an intervention. I started by encouraging the owners to open up about how they were feeling about the sales process up until that point. And once again, they reiterated their fears that the apartment was overpriced and that it would never sell. That's when I told them, "That, right there, is the problem."

They thought I was talking about the price. They were probably pretty shocked when I said, "You have the wrong channel on. I don't even get that channel!"

They looked at me like I was crazy (which is getting to be a theme here, I know). *Wrong channel? What is she talking about?*

I explained a little bit about mindset and told my clients that when they went to bed that night, even if they thought I was crazy, I wanted them to focus on trusting that things would work out. I told them to picture themselves living in their beautiful new apartment. I told them to picture their current apartment selling to a lovely person. And while they might have thought I had completely lost my marbles, at least they agreed to try.

And guess what? Within two weeks, I had an offer for $5,000 over the asking price.

It starts in the mind.

CHAPTER 8

"Would You Like to Hear My Idea for a Show?"

"Be yourself; everyone else is already taken."

—OSCAR WILDE

I love telling stories—if you haven't already figured that out from this book. Maybe because I pay so much attention to the people around me and their behavioral quirks and the other little details that make humans human, I see everything as a story or a movie or at least an *SNL* sketch. People don't just fascinate me; they entertain me—which, I suppose, is part of how I wound up on the TV show *Selling New York*.

Selling New York was a show that aired on HGTV years ago. On *Selling New York*, a predecessor to *Million Dollar Listing*, there was no remodeling because the properties—some of the most luxurious homes and apartments in New York City—were already perfect. It was designed more to be one of those "fly on the wall" experiences, taking viewers inside a world most of them would never see otherwise, peeking behind the curtains of some of the most exclusive real estate in New York City.

One day, one of the producers from *Selling New York* was in my office, filming an episode with a colleague of mine. He was on a break, and we started chatting, and that's when I asked him if he wanted to hear my idea for a show. Of course he did—that's his job, after all—so I shared three stories of things that were really happening in my life, at that time, with my clients and my deals. They were basically three ideas for episodes, although I didn't realize that at the time. But they must have been good ones, because the producer said, "These are amazing. Our biggest struggle is coming up with story lines."

I told him I was a story line addict. "I'm like a faucet that doesn't shut off."

That was all he needed to hear. "Would you be willing to film? What listings do you have?"

I had a townhouse in the West Village, so that became my first episode.

I was already a SAG member (that's the Screen Actors Guild) and dreamed of being an actress or having some kind of career in front of the camera. Well, when I worked on *Selling New York*, I discovered that, while I don't mind being in front of the camera, I actually preferred the behind-the-camera stuff. I loved being creative and didn't mind sharing my own life and career for stories. I loved calling them up and telling them about some client or apartment that I knew would make "good TV." Like, one time, I had just met a woman from Spain, and I showed her a renovated house. After that, I took her to my own apartment, and she decided she liked my place better and wanted to buy it. Oftentimes my experiences wound up with me thinking, *Hey, this would be a great episode.* So I wrote it up and submitted it to the producers, and they said, "Okay, let's shoot that!"

We wound up working really well together. I would write up my little scenarios and send them to the producers, and they would turn them into storylines for the show. The only challenge was when they would try to get me to say things that I wasn't comfortable with—not things that were off-color or anything like that, just ... not authentic to me.

For example, I finished showing a client the inside of a property, and they wanted me to say "Let's go see the roof and party down!"

I was thinking, *You've gotta be kidding.* Anyone watching would know I would *never* say, "party down."

I told them, "Why don't you just roll the camera, and I'll give you something good, and if you don't like it, we'll redo it?" They followed me to the roof-deck, we shot the scene, and it was a wrap.

Thank goodness I avoided becoming the "party down lady." Not that I mind making a fool of myself. I just prefer to keep it real.

Like the day I showed up to the set with two different boots on. It was the best. They panicked.

"She has two different boots on! Keep the camera above the waist."

I said, "It's funny. Show it. This is hilarious, and it's real. Anyone in the industry and every woman is going to relate to this." You know when you put two different shoes on because you're trying to decide which one to wear, and then you get busy and you run out? But they wouldn't go with it. They should have. It would have been so much better.

• • •

I was interviewed to be on the first season of *Million Dollar Listing.* They came to my apartment for a half hour to film me and interview me, and the more I got a sense of what the show was going to be, the less I knew why they were there. I kept saying, "How did you get here?"

The producer said he'd heard I was creative, and that was why they wanted to talk to me.

Then I asked, "What is the show going to be about? Are they going to follow me around every day for six months? Because, I have to be honest with you, I think your ratings may go down if you cast me."

They asked why I thought I'd be such a disappointment.

I said, "Because I'm not going to throw anything at anyone."

I felt they were looking to create a real estate show with the drama of *Real Housewives*. And if you haven't figured it out by now, I'm not that person. If anything, I'm drama averse, especially when it comes to my clients and my career.

But on *Selling New York*, except for the occasionally awkward dialogue and the occasional squabble over commission, they were amazing and let me be me. They certainly didn't expect me to throw a tantrum (or a Jimmy Choo) on screen. In fact, they were so professional they didn't even let my keys hang down from my boots. The whole experience was so much fun, and, for the most part, very comfortable. And the best part was, as people watched me on those episodes, they realized they were watching the real, genuine Vickey. It was kind of like having a promotional video on national TV, and I got to be exactly the same as I was in real life—except for the makeup. That was a big joke with the crew on the show. All the other agents wanted real time to get their hair and makeup done so they looked perfect, like real TV stars, and I would literally say, "I only have twelve minutes. Can we do it fast? I don't care what I look like."

I really don't. Just as long as I don't shine, I'm good.

• • •

Ironically, one of my clients is the makeup artist Laura Mercier. I was helping her pack up her kitchen, and she asked if I knew how we met. Well, I remember everything, so I was sure I did.

I said, "I was showing you an apartment on Eighteenth Street."

But she said, "No, I met you on *Selling New York*"—meaning she didn't *meet* me meet me; she saw me on TV. She went on to explain, "I watched the show, and you were so different. I said to a friend of mine, 'She's real. She's a real human. I connect with her because she doesn't care—not about her hair, not about her makeup. She's just in it, caring about her clients.'" (Should I have been insulted that a professional makeup artist saw me on TV and decided that I don't care about makeup?) "And it was so obvious, watching you, that you were so sincere in your mission to help people that I said, 'I'm going to work with her. She's going to be my agent.' And that's how we started working together."

• • •

The thing is, I really don't know how to be anyone other than myself, even when, maybe, I should try to be. For example, I had been interviewing with the developers of Walker Tower—which, for those of you who are not in real estate, is a classic New York building, first completed in 1929, which they renovated into new, luxury condominiums in 2014. Representing a building like that, with fifty multi-million-dollar apartments, puts you in a different lane in this business, and it's definitely a lane I wanted to be in. So I was fortunate to be interviewing with the developers.

The first question was "Why should we hire you?"

And I said, "I have no idea. I am creative and different, and I definitely don't think like the average bear. I love this building, and I always see the end before the beginning—and I see that this building is a winner."

And then one of the developers asked me to share an example of my creativity. I'm sure they were expecting one of my examples on how I creatively sell out a building, but instead I said, "I just wrote a rap song, if you guys want to hear that."

Yes, I asked two men in an interview if they wanted to hear a rap song I had just written. And maybe because they were too stunned not to, they said, "Okay."

So I launched into my real estate rap song, which I had, honestly, just composed for some reason other than that meeting. It went something like this:

> Brokers, wake up, wake up, wake up.
> Get out of bed. It's way past eight, and you're running late.
> Grab your show sheets, fact sheets, get yourself to Bank Street.
> MetroCard, Crunch Bar, Starbucks too far.
> Ain't got no time for Starbucks.
> You're huffing and you're puffing, and you make it on time
> Just to find your sellers lounging behind …

I finished my song, and the men sat there looking at me—just sitting there, staring at this woman who just performed a rap song in a meeting about a massive real estate project. Interestingly, one of them burst out laughing. We continued our discussion, and they hired me.

What I'm advocating for is not being afraid to be yourself.

Now, am I advocating for you to compose a rap song before your next pitch meeting? Not really, unless you want to … and then, why not? What I'm advocating for is not being afraid to be yourself. I know I'm not better or smarter than other people, but one way I know I'm different is that I'm really comfortable being *me*. I trust myself enough to be myself, and that leaves so much more room in my brain to focus on other people and how I can help them solve their problems—or at least bring them a little unexpected joy.

CHAPTER 9

"Can You Call Up to 14D?"

"A single act of kindness throws out roots in all directions, and the roots spring up and make new trees."

—AMELIA EARHART

I was holding an open house years ago, and some Wall Street guy walked in. He didn't talk much. The apartment was listed at about $535,000 at the time. (Like I said, it was a while ago.) He finished walking around, and said, "Okay, I'll take it." Just like that.

He asked me to call him later with the details, and bought it, just like he said he would. He didn't have a broker with him; he came by himself. But after closing, he said, "Oh, I forgot to tell you something."

"What?"

"I had been working with an agent, and I saw about forty or fifty apartments, but then I walked in your open house, and I liked you, and I liked the apartment, and I just bought it directly with you. My agent wasn't too happy about that. When I told her I already bought an apartment, she said, 'What? You went and bought one without me? After I did all that work? Well, who is the listing agent?' When I said, 'Vickey Barron,' she said, 'Oh, thank goodness. If it was going to be anyone, I'm happy it's her. She is so nice and such a caring person.'"

I thought that was so nice.

But I believe there was a reason why that happened. Six months prior, I had a listing on the Upper East Side. I was in the lobby picking up the key from the doorman when a lady overheard us talking and asked me if I would stop by to look at her apartment after my showing. She shared that she had another agent coming but wanted my thoughts as well. When I came back downstairs to return the key, I noticed an agent in the lobby with listing materials. I could see how enthusiastic she was. It was obvious her belly was turning, and she was so excited at the prospect of getting that listing. At that moment, I felt bad at the thought that I was going to swoop in and potentially take that listing from her. Because her enthusiasm was so contagious, and because I believe in a world of abundance, in that moment I really wanted her to get that listing. I went to the front desk and asked the doorman to call up to 14D. He got the woman on the phone and handed it to me.

I said, "You know what? I'm so sorry. I know I said I'd pop in to talk to you, but I am unfortunately running late, and I've got a lot on my plate, so I'm not going to be able to come up. I'm so sorry." That young agent went up, and guess what? She got the listing, and I was truly happy for her.

If I go and pitch and don't get the listing—because, as I said before, I don't always get every listing—that usually means someone else got it. When that happens, I'll send them a congratulations card or even call them up and say, "I'm so happy for you. I love that home.

If you need anything, let me know. Hopefully I'll have a buyer, but you're going to do a great job."

And people are genuinely puzzled by that. They ask, "Why is she being nice?"

It's sad that a lot of the time, people don't take the time to be nice. They take the time when they're angry to express that. But when they have a chance to call someone and say "Congratulations" or "You looked amazing" or "Thank you," they're too busy, or they feel self-conscious about it, or they just forget about it. And they don't do it.

If that sounds like you, you're missing some amazing opportunities.

It's always been important to me to be nice to people, to spread that little bit of joy, even when maybe they don't deserve it—which brings me back to that Wall Street guy. About a year and a half after he bought the apartment, he called me to sell it. After sending a contract out at full asking price faster than we anticipated, my client called and said, "I know you did all that work, Vickey, but I can't go through with the sale because I don't know where I'm going."

It's always been important to me to be nice to people, to spread that little bit of joy.

I said, "No problem. Don't worry. We'll just find a new buyer."

So I kept going, and, sure enough, three weeks later I found a new buyer. And just when we were ready to send the contract out, my client came back and said, "I can't do it. I'm so sorry. I'm sorry I'm wasting your time."

I said, "Don't worry at all. It must be stressful for you. I know you work a million hours a day."

So I sold the apartment a third time, and this time the market was really in our favor. I raised the price $35,000 and got an offer. Once again, I got contracts and had them signed by the buyer. When it was time for my client to countersign it, he backed out again! This time, he said, "I ... I'm so sorry, but I want to live within a two-block radius, and I have nowhere to go."

At this point, I said, "This is the third time you've changed your mind, but I have more patience than anyone—I can do it fifteen more times. But I feel like all this is putting pressure and causing you anxiety. Why don't we just take your apartment off the market and focus on finding you a place. Then, when we find your new place, we can sell this one. Obviously, I can sell it; I just did it three times."

And he agreed.

Well, everyone in my office was just livid about this:

"You're crazy."

"This is not right."

"You're wasting your time."

"You did all that work, you spent all that money, and now he's not even selling it?"

My feeling was that the energy it would have taken for me to have that debate and argument just wasn't worth it. First of all, I liked him as a person. And second, in that time, I could just go sell another apartment. I was disappointed, but I wasn't angry.

Four weeks later, he called me and said, "Guess what?"

I said, "What?"

"I sold my apartment. My neighbor is buying it, and the best news is I don't have to pay a commission." And then he said, "Do you hate me?"

"I don't hate you. Your brain operates differently than mine, and I don't quite understand that, but I'm happy for you."

And he said, "But now the good news is you can help me find my new place."

Great.

So we started the search. He could only go out at lunch time or after work, and only wanted to see apartments within a two-block radius. I found him something on Park Avenue and sent it over, telling him we could go see it at lunchtime.

No response—which was very unusual for him, at least at that point in the process. Four days went by. I reached out again. He didn't respond. On the sixth day, he called me. "Guess what?"

I said, "What?"

"I found an apartment."

"What? Where?" This had not been an easy search.

He said, "On Park Avenue."

"The one I sent you and said that this was perfect for you?"

"Yup. That one."

"Seriously? I sent that to you."

"Hey, I know you probably hate me. I went in on my own, and I negotiated with the broker directly."

At this point, even if you're not in the real estate business, you probably think I should have hung up on this client and never taken his call again. But that's just not me. So I said, "I don't hate you, but I love that apartment. Don't you love the high ceilings and prewar floors? I love the view. That is the most spectacular apartment."

He said he did.

Then I asked, "When can I come see it? I'm so excited. I'm so happy you got that."

"You don't hate me?"

"No, I want to come see the apartment. Let me know when you close. I'm coming over."

This guy was an avid sailor. So when I came across a sculpture of a ship, I bought it, wrapped it up, and gave it to him. And he looked at me and said, "I can't believe you're not mad. And you're not angry at me?"

I said, "We've already had this conversation. So, you can be as puzzled as you want. I'm not mad at you. I'm just so happy you have this apartment. It's beautiful."

Since then, this one client has referred me close to $30 million in business (and counting). He sent an email last week to some brokers who were trying to cold call him that said, "Vickey Barron is my broker for life. I will never sell my apartment without her."

Even in this cutthroat business, it really does pay to be kind—sometimes, in more ways than one. He has become a friend of the family, and I am happy to have met him.

CHAPTER 10

"What's Your Superpower?"

"The best way to predict the future is to create it."

—ABRAHAM LINCOLN

I didn't write this book just so I could tell a bunch of crazy stories about my life. I certainly have an abundance of them, and it's been a lot of fun remembering them all and writing them down ... but that's still not the reason I took the time to do this. I wrote this book because, every day, somebody asks me what my secret is: how I got where I am, how I do what I do, how I make it look so easy. And honestly, as you've seen in these pages, it's not something I can explain in a few sentences or even over the course of a podcast interview—although I've tried! This is literally the only thing I can think of to get it all down in one place.

I wish I could give you a secret formula to help you get past your fear, loosen up, and trust yourself, but I know that it's easier said than done. Everybody has their own set of superpowers. I guess the secret to my success is a mash-up of six things:

1. Curiosity
2. Creativity
3. Empathic accuracy
4. Hard work
5. Authenticity
6. Passion

When you think about it, none of those things are very hard to do on their own. You just have to figure out where you're getting stuck. If you look at situations from a different angle, or try something new, or do something in a different way, you could wind up discovering your own unique mash-up of superpowers. I swear to you, they're there.

Actually, can I tell you something? There are so many people I meet who are struggling and I wish I could just take them, look them in the eye and magically get them to understand what I know. I wish I could wave a magic wand and just put all this stuff in their head, because it really is so much easier than you think. I get frustrated, sometimes, watching people struggle. It makes me sad for them. And I don't like to be sad. So, of course, I search for a solution—which, I suppose, is the reason why I've been sitting here writing this book.

Considering where I started, I've achieved more than I ever dreamed of achieving, except maybe being a singer. Remember: everything is relative. There are many people who have and will achieve much more than I have. Many of my clients are good examples of that, but I am grateful for my accomplishments.

In 2018, I sat down with Robert Reffkin, Founder and CEO of Compass, to speak about working for his firm. During that discussion, we discovered we are really kindred spirits. He's written his own book on his own amazing journey called *No One Succeeds Alone*, which is incredibly inspirational. We wound up talking about our backgrounds and learned we both come from humble beginnings and were raised by single mothers, so we share a similar worldview. Regardless of how high we are fortunate enough to climb, we both understand that there are all kinds of people in this world, and they all deserve love and respect. We both strive to bring a level of humanity to this business, which is part of why I feel so privileged to work with Robert. Watching him give back to the community and his agents resonates with me because sharing what I've learned in real estate and in life with the next generation brings me joy. I love to see them light up as they find the same kind of fulfillment in this business that I have.

• • •

Giving back feels good to me. It has ever since I watched my mother open her heart to every struggling soul who was lucky enough to cross her path. It's watching a person's whole demeanor change when they see that someone cares. So today, I try to give back.

For decades, I've been in awe of an organization called Pathways to Independence, which my good friend Gayle introduced me to. She actually held the first meeting in her living room many years ago. The mission of Pathways to Independence is to transform the lives of disadvantaged single young women—through education, therapy, mentoring, housing, and healthcare—to break the cycle of poverty and abuse.

Living across the country, I don't donate one zillionth the amount of time or energy that Gayle and others do, but I try to support the organization however I can, including the time I got a client to let us use his private plane for a fundraiser. Also, by giving Pathways a shout-out in my book because they deserve it.

Pathways speaks to me because it supports women who don't have resources, love, or support. I didn't have a lot growing up, but I did have a clean, safe home and a mom who loved me, taught me independence and to dream big. And that made all the difference for me. It gave me the foundation I needed to build a successful life. Pathways provides that foundation to women who are homeless or in recovery or in difficult family situations, giving them the help and guidance they don't get from their families or schools or communities. It works because it's not just a handout; it's giving people the tools to change their situation permanently and build successful lives. As long as they stay in school, working toward a degree and maintaining a good GPA, the women are provided with housing and medical care, as well as the psychological support they need to stay on track. It's an amazing organization that lifts up so many women, and I'm proud to be associated with it, even a little bit.

• • •

Most of the volunteering I do, however, I do in New York, working with my fellow agents. Even though I don't like focusing on my accomplishments, one honor that really means a lot to me is the Real Estate Board of New York's Eileen Spinola Award for Distinguished Service. I received that award for the work I do with agents from all firms. I give talks and teach classes, and mentor agents, all to pass on what I know. Whether it is to help someone find their spark or survive a rough patch if they need it.

I truly love the work, although, like a lot of the things I do, some people think I'm crazy for doing it. They're always asking me, "Why do you spend all those hours volunteering?" Or the question that's the hardest for them to wrap their heads around: "Why are you up there sharing your secrets?"

Honestly? I do it because, as I said before, it makes me feel good to help people. And it's not like I'm the only person in the room worth listening to. Every time I'm up there, I benefit from the experience. There's a whole new generation out there that knows things I definitely don't. I can meet an agent who's been in the business for one week, and I will learn something new from that agent. Why would I deprive myself of those opportunities?

As for sharing my secrets, I'm more than happy to. I know we're all supposed to be each other's competition, but after everything I've experienced in my life, I can't help believing that we live in a world of abundance. There's enough business to go around. Why not share that energy and help one another? When I'm in that classroom and agents come up to me after the class, or I see them a month later or a year later, and they say, "Vickey! There was something you shared that helped **I really believe that every agent is my partner—I don't care what firm they're at.** me get a listing. There's a tip you provided me that helped me in a negotiation," that just feels good. Because, at the end of the day, we're all in this together.

I really believe that every agent is my partner—I don't care what firm they're at—and without them, I cannot succeed. Getting an award recognizing my contributions to our industry means a lot, but this industry, and the people I've met through it, has given me so much more than I've given it.

So now that we're reaching the end of the book, I'm turning the last few chapters over to you. I've shared what makes me tick, how I operate, some of the questions I've asked that have helped me get where I am, and some stories that I imagine have you questioning my sanity. Now, I want to move to the questions people ask me (which don't necessarily involve my sanity). Hopefully you'll find some answers to your own questions or at least some good ideas.

CHAPTER 11

"How Do You Deal with Failure?"

"I have not failed. I've just found ten thousand ways that won't work."

—THOMAS EDISON

A lot of people have the mistaken impression that I never fail. In fact, the exact opposite is true. To some, I may be a so-called successful person, but I fail *all the time*. And I've been doing it for as long as I can remember.

I couldn't speak properly until I was six or seven, so, right off the bat, nobody had much confidence I would amount to much of anything. My teachers agreed; I had to do first grade twice, (Yes, I failed first grade.), and things didn't get much better when I got older. In seventh grade, I was in the middle of choir rehearsal when the teacher moved me to the last row. She pulled me aside the next day and said it was okay if I stayed in choir but only if I lip-synched. The following year, I was in a French class, about one month into the semester, and the teacher asked me to stay after class. He told me he spoke to another teacher about me, and—"Good news!"—there was an opening for me in home economics class. I took the hint, language was not my strong suit.

However, there was a silver lining to the cloud of my limited abilities and questionable skills: it taught me to work hard. Despite losing a year in first grade, I managed to graduate a year early, because

> **So today, I welcome failure—which is a good thing, because I haven't stopped failing yet.**

I spent every moment I could on my studies. I remember senior ditch day, when the only people who showed up for class were me and a girl with Coke-bottle glasses. I learned that by working hard, you can overcome failure—not that that will always keep it from happening. I still failed over and over, and it didn't kill me. It just pushed me to be better. So today, I welcome failure—which is a good thing, because I haven't stopped failing yet.

Here's a recent example. I showed up for a panel I was doing for an audience of about a hundred people. I started looking for my name tag on the table of panelists, and I didn't see it. I started thinking maybe it was the wrong day or the wrong panel ... when my eyes drifted over to the podium, and I saw my name—on the podium— meaning I wasn't on the panel. I was supposed to *moderate* the panel.

Oops.

When you're the moderator of a panel, you have to be prepeared. You have to understand the topic that's going to be discussed, and know what questions you're going to ask. It's a completely different role than being on a panel. I (yes me, of all people) found myself for the first time ever without a question, as I didn't realize I was supposed to moderate this panel. In other words, I had messed up big-time.

My heart was pounding, but I had to go up there and moderate. It wasn't like they could call someone else up there to do it. And as bad as I might look doing it, it would look even worse if I didn't show up at all. So even though I was panicking and not prepared, I took action.

Specifically, I took a napkin and quickly wrote down the names of the people who were on the panel. I knew what the topic was (luckily!), so I kicked off the panel by asking one of the agents a general question about the topic. Then, to give myself time to think of the next question, I paused and said, "Ladies and gentlemen, did you hear what Raphael just said? Interesting, isn't it?" Then I turned to the next panelist and said, "Michelle, can you talk to me about what Raphael said?" Instead of panicking to come up with my next question, I really listened to what they were saying and was able to build on their answers and engage the audience. We wound up having a great and smooth discussion. It worked out really well but only because—even though I had made a big, giant mistake—I didn't get bogged down in analysis paralysis. I trusted myself despite all evidence to the contrary, took a deep breath, and moved forward.

And you know what? When I was done, people came up to me and said, "You're an amazing moderator. You should do this more often." All I could think was, *If they only knew ...*

So, what is "analysis paralysis"? That's when you're so busy thinking through the potential consequences of making a move that you never actually make it, and the moment passes you by. It affects a lot of people in a lot of different situations—and I see it in real estate agents all the time.

It's so sad. Every day, they come in fully intending to kill it. They get all dressed up in their best professional clothes. They sit down at their desks and get on the phone and give it their all. But they don't make movement. They don't get anywhere. Maybe that's why the average real estate agent sells two to five properties a year. Now, I don't know about you, but I need to sell more than two to five properties a year to live.

Still, if you're doing everything you can and nothing's happening, I can promise you it isn't happening to you because you're terrible at your job. It could be happening because you're trying too hard to be perfect at your job.

Maybe you're so busy waiting until you know every answer and have every *t* crossed and every *i* dotted before you take action that you never *do*, or by the time you do, it's too late. If that sounds like you, you probably fear failure. And the sad thing about that is your fear of failure is actually the thing that makes you fail. With that said, it is up to you to constantly challenge yourself and continue to learn and grow.

Take it from a woman who has failed numerous times: success isn't about being perfect. If it was, I would have been out of this business long ago. It's about trusting yourself and your ability to figure things out as you go. If I waited until I knew everything—

- if I didn't pursue that first For Sale by Owner listing, even though the woman I called for my homework assignment wasn't very nice to me;
- if I didn't hold my own against the aggressive guy who put his finger in my face and asked why he should trust me when I'd only been in business for two weeks (well, I might have just run away after that one!);
- if I had let my fear or other people's moods or opinions get in the way of what I was trying to do (which was help these people!)

—I never would have become Rookie of the Year, and you probably wouldn't be reading this book right now.

Since I didn't have experience, I focused on the things I knew I did have, like the ability to take care of people and to work hard. I trusted that, as long as I kept my focus on those two things, the rest of it would work itself out. I promise you—speaking as an imperfect person who forgets names, shows up to moderate a panel without questions, doesn't always bring numbers to a big developer meeting, and plenty of other things I haven't mentioned in this book—it will work itself out for you too. You don't have to be perfect as long as you always try to do your best for the people you're working for.

By the way, it's also okay not to have every answer. It's okay to say "I have no idea. That's an excellent question. Let me get back to you." In fact, the *worst* thing to do when you don't know something is to make up some answer that's incorrect, or lie, or not even be present in the situation and just let it float away. It's always better to understand and grow by allowing yourself to fail. After all, how else are you going to know where you need to grow?

Learn from failure. Push past it. And it can be your biggest teacher. It has definitely been one of mine.

CHAPTER 12

"How Do You Handle Rejection?"

"Success is buried on the other side of rejection."

—TONY ROBBINS

What's even scarier than failure? Rejection. People really, really hate rejection—which makes real estate extra challenging, because in real estate we face it all the time. We're all losing listings or buyers to other agents. It's a fact of this business.

It's just not the fact I focus on.

That became painfully obvious when I started this book. I planned to give you a full picture of my career, missteps and all, including the times I've been rejected. But a funny thing happened when I sat down at the computer: every time I tried to remember a specific story, I couldn't zero in on any details, or the story wound up unfolding in a way where things worked out.

Of course I've lost clients and I've had failures but what is important is how we bounce back. After learning from these mistakes,

I choose to store these experiences in the back of the filing cabinet, not the front—and I'm aware of them, and I can retrieve them if needed. But I guess the question is, Why would I continue to revisit them? What good is it to play that record over and over again about how I failed and everything is terrible? Instead of focusing on that loss, I'd rather hold on to the lesson learned and go sell another apartment or help another individual. I suppose that's why so many of my rejection stories end up with a happy ending. I don't let it stop me. The victim mentality is a handicap that I see in people far too often. My suggestion is to stop blaming other people.

Honestly, why worry about one rejection when there are plenty of homes to sell? There's an abundance. They're everywhere. There are not enough hours in the day to sell them all. Keep going. There's plenty to achieve. If you go to a pitch and lose a listing, just keep pitching. Eventually you're going to get a listing.

• • •

Another thing I do when I lose a listing, which you might think is a little crazy, is instead of worrying and beating myself up over it, I congratulate the agent who got it.

For example, I was working with another agent on a $40 million-plus listing, and it went off the market for a bit while the owner dealt with some other issues. When he was ready to put the property back on the market, he called me and told me he had decided that instead of working with Agents A and B, as he had when the property was listed before, he was just going to go with Agent A.

I was Agent B in this scenario. Basically, the guy was firing me.

But I didn't get upset, or ask why or if there was anything else I could do, or get angry or even sad. I actually thought my now-former client was really gracious to call me and have a personal conversation, instead of emailing me or leaving a message at my office. Not everyone would be so considerate, but he was actually concerned about how I was going to feel about his decision. I thanked him for taking the time out of his busy schedule to call me.

"What's most important is that you feel that you're in the right hands," I said. "And what I'm hearing is that you feel that Agent A is going to be more successful selling it solo. And you're asking me to step aside. Is that correct?"

He told me he was.

I said, "I will step aside. And by the way, I think the world of Agent A; you are in excellent hands. And at any time, should they have any questions or if I can help on the sideline, by all means, I'm here to support both of you."

When I hung up with my now-former client, I called Agent A and congratulated him. I said, "I'm so happy for you. It's a beautiful apartment. You're going to knock it out of the ballpark."

Guess what happened next? Agent A immediately called the owner to tell the owner that I responded the way I did. The owner said, "She's unbelievable. She's just so gracious."

Now, was I disappointed that I didn't get that listing? One hundred percent. But this was the owner's decision, and my job is to serve the owner. So why not support Agent A, wish him the very best, and do anything I could to assist him to help that owner get to the finish line?

Seriously. Why not? What did I have to lose, seeing as I'd already lost the listing?

Instead, I gained so much. The owner felt good that I wasn't upset and there were no hard feelings. Agent A felt good that I was supportive and happy for him, and I felt good that, at the end of the day, I had strengthened two relationships, my reputation, and made two human beings' lives a little bit easier. In fact, I've done multiple transactions with Agent A and this client since that time.

The times when things go wrong are just as important—or even more important—to building strong relationships as the times when things go right. That's when people's true colors show. And honestly, is giving someone the stink eye ever a winning plan in the end? We're all adults here. Everyone has to eat. Everyone deserves a chance to work. You don't have to pick up every single crumb. Sometimes, you do more for yourself by helping somebody else. If you do the right thing, it all comes back to you.

> **And honestly, is giving someone the stink eye ever a winning plan in the end?**

Whatever you do, you gain nothing by beating yourself up over rejection. If the worst thing happens is you lose (which you will), trust that, for whatever reason, it was a blessing in disguise, and move on. And with the example of the lost listing, you can go the extra step to help that person. For example, if you have some great historical information about the listing, share it with the agent, and they're going to be shocked when you offer to help them. But pretty soon, people won't be shocked because generosity will become part of your reputation and your brand.

And that's worth more than a $40 million listing.

CHAPTER 13

"How Do You Deliver Bad News?"

"So often in life things that you regard as an impediment turn out to be great good fortune."

—RUTH BADER GINSBURG

I have this fantasy about starting a dating site where everyone is completely, 100 percent honest. Instead of taking one hundred selfies to get one at the perfect angle where your double chin doesn't show and using a filter on your face to blur the lines, why not just say "I have some wrinkles … I snore at night … I have a muffin top"? That kind of honesty would save a lot of people uncomfortable moments later. And why not? Reality is reality. You can lie about it. You can hide it. But eventually, it's gonna catch up with you.

That's not a problem for me because I happen to be a bad-news specialist. In fact, some of my colleagues actually call me that.

Ever since I was telling doctors about the low pay and expensive housing on Guam and Saipan (while trying to get them to move there!), I've been a master at delivering news people don't want to hear. I'm always very upfront about the bad news and deliver it first, pointing out the challenges to get them out of the way. Then I wrap my arms around something positive and take it from there.

• • •

I recently sold a unit in a building with a really unattractive school across the street. The situation was not good. Everyone would come in and say, "Oh, I love the building, but that *school!*"

And I would say, "Yeah, I tried to move it, but it's not going anywhere. Wait till you see the kids coming out of it. They're not a picnic either." But after addressing the elephant in the room (or, more accurately, across the street from the room), I also said, "But somehow, it's not stopping people from buying in here. Let me show you the lobby." Then I took the buyers in and talked about the beautiful building. Because I was honest about the reality that there was an ugly school full of rowdy kids across the street from the building I was showing them, they trusted me.

My clients trust that I will take care of them. They feel safe with me, like they would with their doctor. In the middle of the pandemic, when sales were down in New York City, my sales (at least the number of sales) were up—because my clients trusted me to get them through a difficult time, when prices were plummeting and people were fleeing the city.

• • •

So, why is the way you deliver bad news so important? Look at it this way. Imagine you need to tell your client that a third deal blew up and the buyer's not going to sign the contract. You have to be the one to deliver that bad news. So you call that client and say, "Mr. Seller, I'm so sorry. I didn't sleep all night. I have a stomachache. I can't believe this happened. I feel so bad." That's what a lot of agents would say in this situation. They'd tell the seller how sorry they are and how bad they feel.

Now imagine you walk into a doctor's office for some test results, and you hear "Oh my gosh, I am so sorry. I didn't see this coming. I got the results. It's bad. It's really bad. I didn't sleep all night. I have a stomachache thinking about it." You'd freak out—and hopefully get a second opinion from a doctor who wasn't in the middle of a nervous breakdown!

You want to hear the doctor say, "We have a plan. You're going to come back on Tuesday. We're going to do X, Y, and Z." What clients want from

Emotional thinking and logical thinking together add up to wise thinking.

agents is no different. They want you to say, "Listen. That deal fell apart. I've already called the two backups. We have an open house scheduled for Sunday. I'm going to do this. I'm going to do that, and we will get to the finish line."

When you approach delivering bad news this way, with a plan for moving forward and getting to your destination, it keeps you in control. It shows you have a strategy. This is a bump in the road, but you're going to get them to the end. I'm not saying you can't show emotion—you're human, and it's okay to feel things, as long as you pair those feelings with logical thinking. Emotional thinking and logical thinking together add up to wise thinking.

Learning to deliver bad news is especially important in real estate when we have to deliver bad news right up front—like when you meet with an owner about a listing, and they tell you they need to sell for X number of dollars. However, because it's your job to know the market and you have more information than your client, you know there's no way the home will sell for that price.

When that happens, it can feel like you're in a bind. If you tell the prospective client no, that you don't see their property the way they see it and that the market won't support what they want, you might lose the listing. That's why a lot of agents just give in and give the client what they want and call it "customer service." But how is it a service to a customer to list at a price you know is too high and just hope and pray you're wrong, a miracle will happen, and someone will buy it before your client gives up and lists with someone else?

Since I'm the bad-news specialist, I, of course, have my own way of dealing with this kind of situation. First of all, I've always done my research, so I have complete trust in my numbers and can confidently represent them that way. As the expert in the situation, I need to be honest with my clients, or I'm not doing my job. But, at the same time, it's also my job to try to get the client what they want. So when someone tells me they *need* something, that's when I start asking questions. I try to figure out what they *really* need or what is going on behind the scene so I can help them meet their goals the best way I can.

In all honesty, I would rather lose a listing if I don't believe in it. But of course I have clients who really, really want to list at a higher price than I would advise. When that happens, my next step is to propose a compromise. I usually say something like, "I will give it my all at that number for thirty days. At the end of thirty days, let's look at the data, study it, and see if we're going in the right direction, because I don't want you to chase the number downward. And that's what can happen. You can end up with less money if we go in the wrong direction. Does that make sense to you?"

They usually say yes. And then I go on and, more often than not, end up adjusting the price to sell their property. And I do it knowing I deserve their trust.

CHAPTER 14

"How Do You Become a Top Agent?"

"Strive not to be a success, but rather to be of value."

—ALBERT EINSTEIN

The examples in this chapter are about real estate; however, these strategies and mindsets will help you succeed in whatever profession you are in. I know I keep saying I don't like to talk about numbers or awards or the titles I've been given over the years. And really, I don't. I only put accolades on my website and business cards because it matters to other people.

There is one stat that I am proud to talk about: over the last twenty-plus years, between 93 and 96 percent of my business has been referral, which means my clients trust me enough to tell their friends and families about me.

In life, people are going to talk about you. The question is, What do you want them to say? When I lost that $40 million listing to Agent A, I could have lost my mind, or I could have been the person

I am, who's basically allergic to drama. As you've probably noticed in this book, there have been many, many occasions where I could have gotten angry or complained or bad-mouthed someone all over town. You might even think some of those people deserved it. I guess I'm lucky I'm just not wired that way; I think people deserve to feel good, not bad. I want to leave them feeling happy and positive. Maybe that's kept me from burning some bridges another person in my position might have torched.

At the end of the day, I think being a top agent is about hard work and getting out of your own way. If you take the attention off of you and put it on your client, care about them, and make sure every decision you make is for their benefit, they will at least recognize your actions, and they will talk about you, and recommend you.

That, honestly, is how I got here—by getting out of my own way and making it not about me.

• • •

Real estate is a complex field. I can't think of another line of work that combines such high financial stakes with such high emotional stakes. A home may be a lot of people's biggest asset, but beyond that, it's their *home*. It's where they celebrate milestones and dream their dreams. It's the stage where people's lives play out. So, when you deal with people's homes, you're dealing with a part of them, really. It's not just a commodity, and it's not just about the money. It's about their life and who they are. Maybe the reason so many people have trusted me over the years is that I get that. Selling houses is about a person or a family and their home—and helping everyone find their own movie ending.

You'd never know that from the way most agents market themselves. I keep seeing agents who seem to feel the need to make themselves into a human infomercial—like they need to be bigger than life and show the world that they're the greatest real estate agent that ever walked the earth, or at least the streets of New York City. It's fine to be proud of your accomplishments, but I've never understood how or why this would appeal to a seller. How is some slick marketing campaign about how great you are going to help somebody sell their home?

I was selling a townhouse once, and I made a little book about the house—the whole house, with pictures and information and everything a person who might want to buy that house would want to know. My contact information was on the back, along with a little picture of me, so a person would know who to call if they were interested, but the house was the subject of the book, not Vickey Barron. I didn't make a book about me. Yes, this book you're reading is a book about me, but I'm not using it to try to sell somebody's house. I'm using it to try to help *you* sell somebody's house or several houses. Or, if you are not in real estate, hopefully this recipe has value in your field of interest.

People do the same thing when they pitch themselves for listings. For twenty minutes, they'll sit in front of a human being who needs their help with a very complex thing, and they'll spend nineteen of those minutes talking about themselves, their record of sales, and how well they treat their clients. Instead, they could use those twenty minutes to demonstrate how well they treat their clients by asking their potential clients—who are sitting right in front of them!—questions about the problem they need them to solve: What are their goals? What are they worried about? What matters to them?

That's why, when I sit down with a prospective client to talk about a listing, I don't waste time on my numbers or awards. Nobody wants to hear about me and my record and my success. They want to know how I'm going to sell their house. That's what people wanted from me before I ever had a record of success, and it's what they want today. It's what they want from you too. You don't need a fancy title or a lot of awards; I had neither of those things when I started out.

That doesn't mean this approach is going to work with everyone all the time. Some people really do care about the "trappings" of success. But I still approach them the same way. I can only be who I am. There was one time when I almost didn't get a townhouse listing because someone I was pitching against pointed out to the owner that I had a studio listed for sale on my website for $350,000. This townhouse was $7.5 million, and the owner just could not wrap her head around her beautiful, luxurious townhouse appearing on the same website as a $350,000 studio. She told me, "I'm kind of torn because I want to hire you, but the other agent is a vice president, and she only sells exclusive, high-end townhouses." My card only said I was an associate salesperson, which I guess she found much less impressive and reinforced whatever bad feelings the $350,000 studio brought up.

I said, "Thank you so much for bringing that up. The truth of the matter is, when I got my license, I said to myself, 'I never want to be the individual that is too busy or too important not to help everybody.' So if you have a niece or nephew moving to the city who needs their first-time studio, as much as I like helping the $20+ million buyer, it feels good to help that first-time buyer. So I really do thank you for noticing that on my website and I hope ten years from now, you'll still see that on my website."

My speech must have been effective, because the woman did end up hiring me despite my lack of a fancy title and willingness to list entry-level properties. I went back to my firm and told the story to my manager, and he said, "Well, Vickey, you *are* a senior vice president—

with your numbers." Apparently, rank was decided by numbers at our firm, and mine were high enough to make me a senior vice president.

So I called my new client back and told her. "Apparently I'm a senior vice president, but I didn't know that was a thing."

So, yes, she got what she wanted. But it wasn't why she hired me in the first place.

• • •

I get that you still might not be convinced of my approach, especially since you know my credentials and track record. But remember I wasn't always at this level. I was once a newbie who was just learning to master the subway when I started, and I achieved Rookie of the Year. That's why I know this stuff works. I've been trying to explain that this approach works ever since I tried to help my sales team have fun selling health plans door to door.

I know how hard it can be sometimes to let go and trust that it will all work out. (That's why I wish I had that magic wand to wave!) I know it can be scary to think of *not* talking about how great you are during a pitch. The agent who came in before you probably talked about how great they are, and the one after you will too. I promise if you are authentic to who you are, demonstrate your value, and ask intelligent questions, you will stand out.

If you are ever in doubt, just imagine yourself sitting in the doctor's office and the door opens, and instead of them asking you health-related questions (like if you've ever smoked, blood pressure, family history, etc.), they stood in front of you and spent that time touting what school they went to, where they were ranked, and that they were written up in the *New England Journal of Medicine* ten times. If they did that, it would probably be alarming. Realistically, you probably looked up their credentials beforehand or had them referred to you, so this valuable time should be spent on them caring for you.

You can probably see how silly this sounds, hopefully.

If you've ever read a sales book or taken a sales course of any kind, you've heard that phrase "Show, don't tell." When you ask the right kind of questions, you *show* your client how great you are by letting them see exactly how you would work with them.

There's one major caveat here. You can't achieve this just by asking a bunch of random questions. In the classes I teach, I actually tell people *not* to ask questions if they don't understand what they're going to do with the answer. A doctor doesn't send a patient in for a test if they don't know what they want to do with the results. When you ask a potential client a question, it should have value. If you're just asking questions and the answers have no meaning, and you don't really understand why you're asking the questions in the first place, those are not good questions. You need to ask questions for the sole purpose of discovery which will help you get on the right path to help them.

You don't just launch into another question, you wait for a response and listen to what the client says because the answer has importance to you. So when you ask your next question, it's related to that response and moves you a little further down the path. You do it again and again, until you're having a conversation about your client's goals, demonstrating your skills by showing them you care about them and their needs.

I don't even stop when I get the listing. If I'm working with someone, I really want to know who they are. I listen and watch constantly, and I take mental notes. If we go out to lunch and they mention they don't drink coffee, only tea, I'll make that note. If they say, "I'm addicted to chocolate," and I find myself in the ultimate chocolate store, I'll send them a treat. However, if they're gluten-free and you are aware, you are not going to send them a fresh box of croissants. I'll make note of their spouse's name, their children's names. If they have a pet, I'll even jot down the pet's name. But it's not a stretch for me. I find people of interest. I like people. So part of the fun of my job is getting to know them.

I spend a lot of energy and time with the people that I work with. If you have bought or sold a house or an apartment with me, you're kind of stuck with me for life. I don't go away. I do not give closing gifts, for whatever that's worth. I think it's really awkward, although I know some people do it very successfully. So if it works for you, go for it. I don't do it because I become a part of my clients' lives. I sprinkle them with unique gifts and notes throughout the year and for years to come. And I stay in contact with them, and I remember what matters to them.

> **The bottom line is that we're in a business where our job is to serve other people.**

For example, I had a client who was an amazing pianist. I saw this beautiful scarf with piano keys all over it, and it reminded me of her. So I bought it and sent it with a note. I send a lot of handmade cards and notes, and I'm just constantly touching the people that I've worked with. As a result, I think they first see me as Vickey Barron, who happens to sell real estate, instead of my real estate agent who happens to be Vickey Barron.

The bottom line is that we're in a business where our job is to serve other people. They don't care what our title is or what our agenda is. They don't care that we want to make our numbers work or get a commission check to pay our mortgage. They don't care about that.

They care about their situation and their needs, and we are there to find out what those needs are and service them.

As soon as you go in with that mentality—that you're there to help and serve; that you need to ask questions to better understand what this person's needs are; and that *This is going to be fun, and together we can get to the finish line*—then, all of a sudden, you separate yourself from the rest. All of a sudden, you're no longer a salesperson; you're a human with a strategy to help them accomplish something that's really, really important to them.

Of course, there are still a few other things you need to do to reach top-agent status besides asking questions. You need to actually work hard. You shouldn't be above cleaning up cat vomit (like I did with one of my very first listings) or making a bed, if that's what your client needs in a particular moment. And you need to educate yourself. Before my license was even valid, I used to spend countless hours going to open houses, taking notes. I was always curious. *Why was this one priced at that price versus this price? What makes one more valuable than the other?* I spent hours studying all that stuff because it genuinely fascinated me. Honestly, if you're not interested in what you're doing, maybe you're in the wrong business, but if you approach things with curiosity, if you're passionate with a desire to learn, you will keep getting better and better because you will keep learning more and more.

So, how do you become a top agent? If you work hard, are present, remove your ego, have integrity, focus on serving other people, ask questions to help you do that, and, most importantly, talk less and listen more, you'll do just fine.

CHAPTER 15

"How Do You Not Take Yourself So Seriously?"

"You're braver than you believe, and stronger than you seem, and smarter than you think."

—A. A. MILNE

Now you know a little bit about how I got from Long Beach, California, to that penthouse on the High Line, and all the other amazing places I've been, thanks to the work I've done. My story isn't what most people expect. They are honestly surprised to learn I come from humble beginnings, but I wouldn't have it any other way. That's how I learned that, no matter where you grew up or what you do for a living, treat people with kindness. It's where I learned my work ethic and discovered how much joy I can get just bringing other people happiness. It's where I learned to meet people where they're at, to listen to what they have to say, and to focus on offering whatever I can to help solve whatever problem they have—skills that have not only helped me in business but might have saved my life on more than one occasion.

Maybe this all hasn't added up to what you expected from a so-called "real estate book." There was no one supersecret formula for winning the listing or getting the highest offer or any step-by-step guide to take you from point A to point Z, although I did try to share a few of my methods and walk you through a few scenarios. But after reading an entire book about me (and thank you so much for that, by the way), you've probably figured out that doing the thing people expect isn't really what I'm about—which reminds me of one last story I haven't told yet …

• • •

A few years back, I was referred to a buyer named Michael, who was looking for an apartment for himself and his partner in a new development. He was clearly creative, artistic, and successful, but since he was referred to me by a reliable source, I didn't do the typical background check, and I was not clear on what he did for a living. I was focused on rolling out the red carpet and identifying what apartment may be the right fit.

Anyway, I was in the elevator with Michael, heading up to show him one of the apartments, when, all of a sudden, I felt this overwhelming urge to *sing*.

I should remind you I am *not* a singer. Remember the choir story? You will not be seeing me on *The Voice* anytime soon. However, in my heart of hearts, I really *wish* I could sing. I wish it so much. The fact that I'm not very good at it doesn't stop me from doing it, so I do.

We were riding up in the elevator and I suddenly looked at my client, Michael, and said, "Can I ask you a question?"

He nodded.

"Would you like me to sing for you right now?" He looked at me and said, "Go for it." (I knew I had a captive audience.)

Now, again—I can't stress this enough—I'm really, *really* bad at singing. I can make dogs howl. But I kept a straight face, and I sang my little heart out. I can't remember the song, but I do remember Michael standing there, looking at me with this slightly bemused expression on his face, probably desperately waiting for the elevator to arrive at our floor and put him out of his misery.

A couple days later, I was showing a different apartment to Michael (who thankfully did not fire me after hearing me sing). This time, we were with his partner, and we entered a room that was full of photographs of famous musicians and pretty much everyone who was ever anyone in the music business. Then Michael's partner pointed to a photo, chuckled, and said, "Hey, Michael, look! Small world. We are having dinner with them tonight."

Aha! They must be in the music industry!

But still, who were they? The truth of the matter is I've been fortunate to work with many different celebrities over the years, but I'd be lying if I said I knew who all of them were initially. I guess I should spend more time reading *People* magazine. When I went back downstairs, I checked the log where we signed in to go up to see the apartment. I saw Michael's last name.

And then it hit me: *That* Michael! I love his songs!

Figuring out who he was made the whole thing even funnier. He probably thought I was trying to get discovered or something. But honestly, I was just really having fun.

• • •

And that, in a nutshell, is what I want for you. Work takes up so much of our lives that it's just not worth it if you're not having fun.

I knew that when I was an eighteen-year-old kid selling healthcare plans door to door, and I knew it as a Manhattan broker who decided to sing to a rock star (albeit without knowing it!) in an elevator. If you can't find joy in your work—if it's painful, torturous, or even just boring—maybe it's not the right work for you. Or maybe you need to rethink how you're approaching it.

So open your heart, open your mind, remember to be kind, and, most of all, have fun.